This Coloring Book Belongs to:

Copyright 2021 SID's Creative Room Books
Author & Illustrator: Szidónia Pethő (Sid)
www.szidoniapetho.com

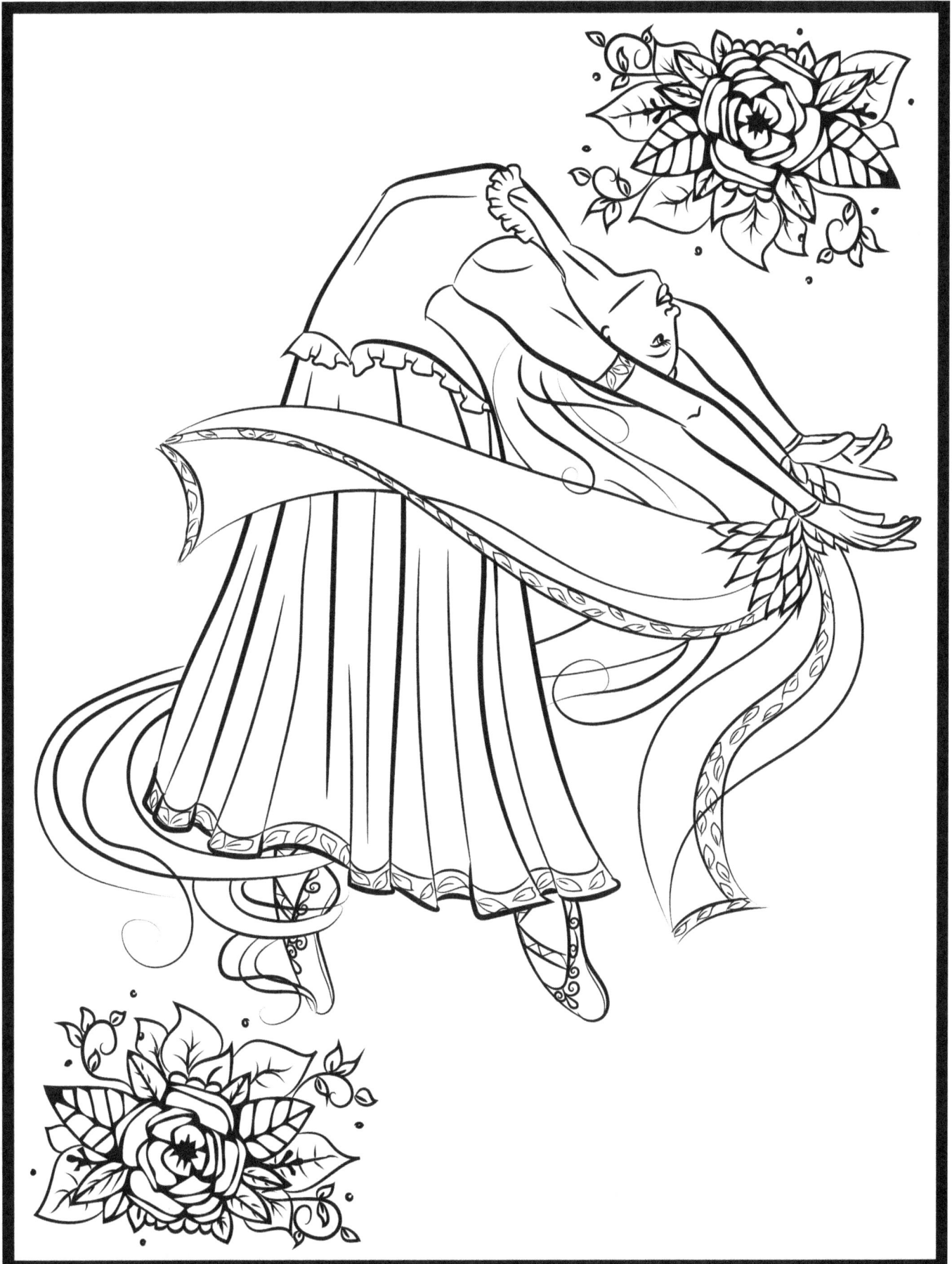

Autumn Dance

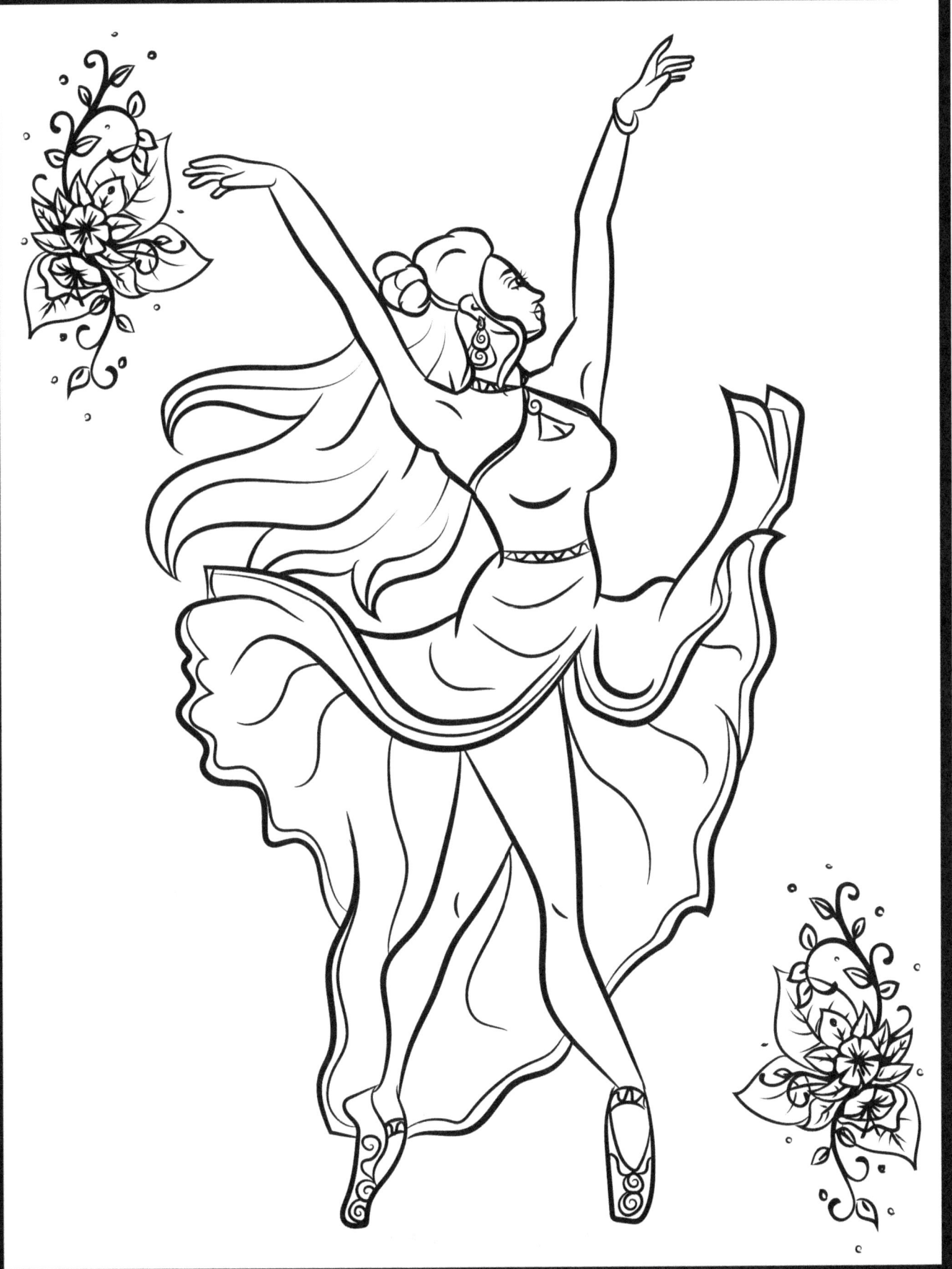

Floral Freedom

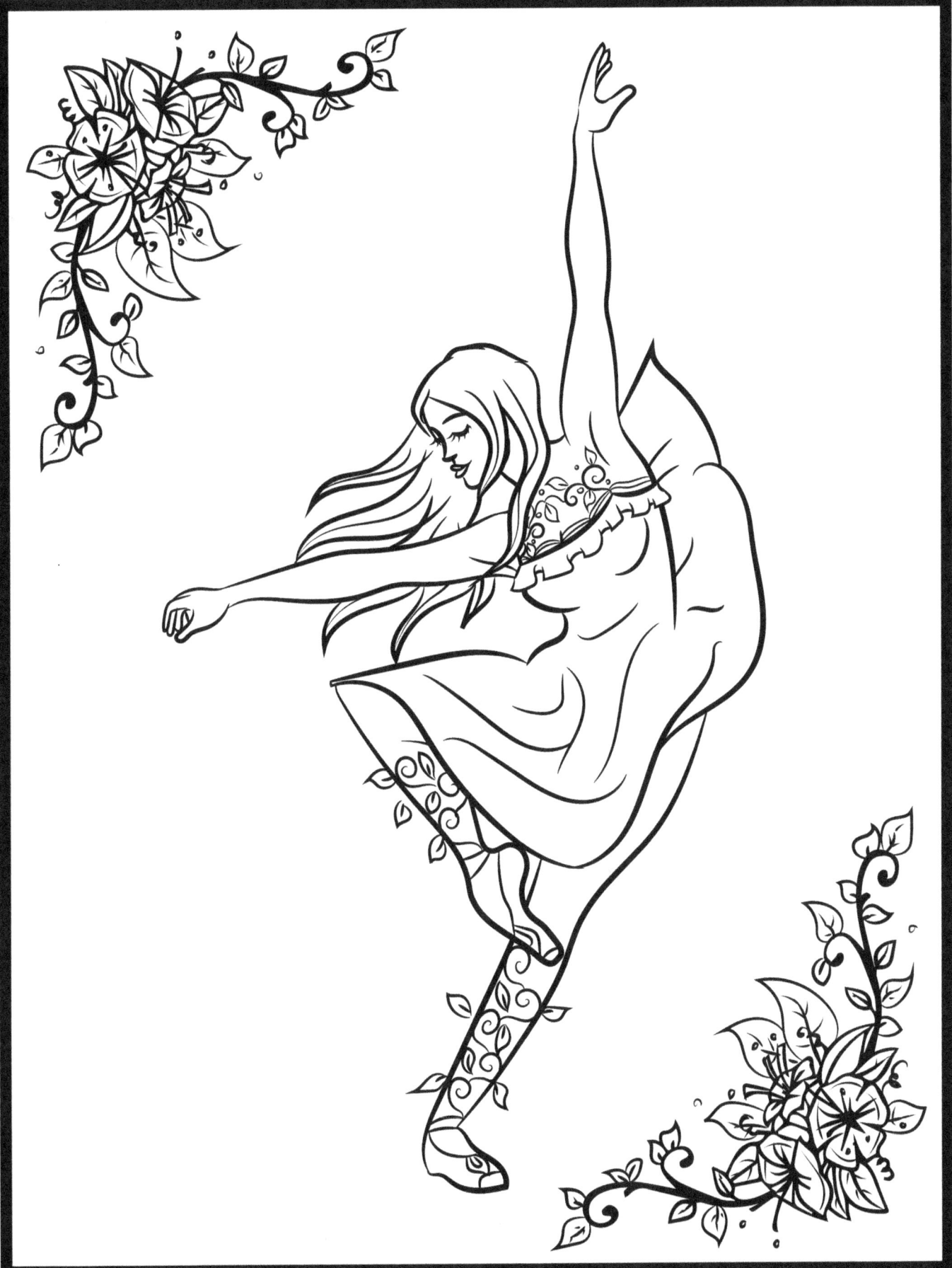

Sound of Innocence

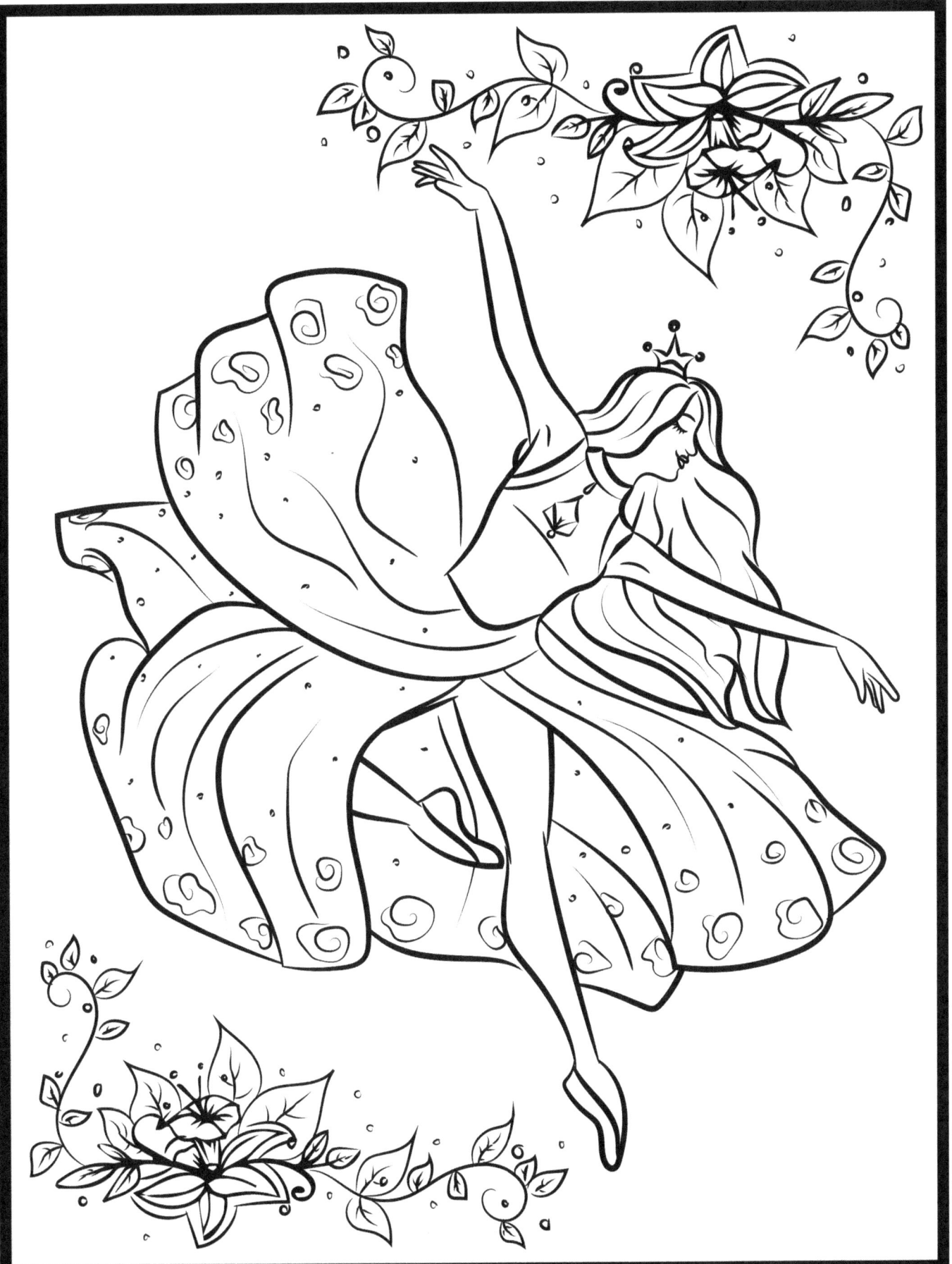

Royal Heart

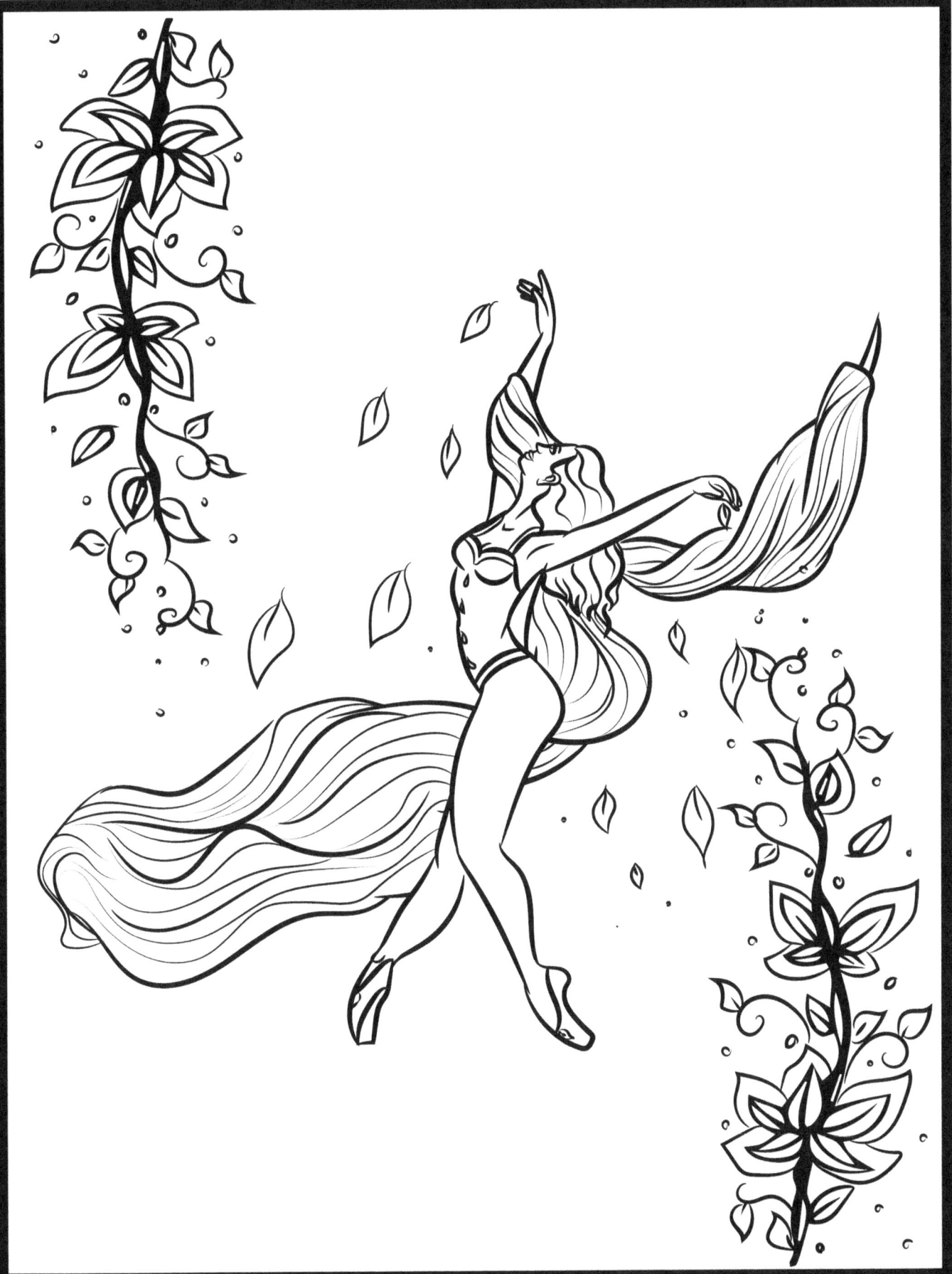

Spring Ballet

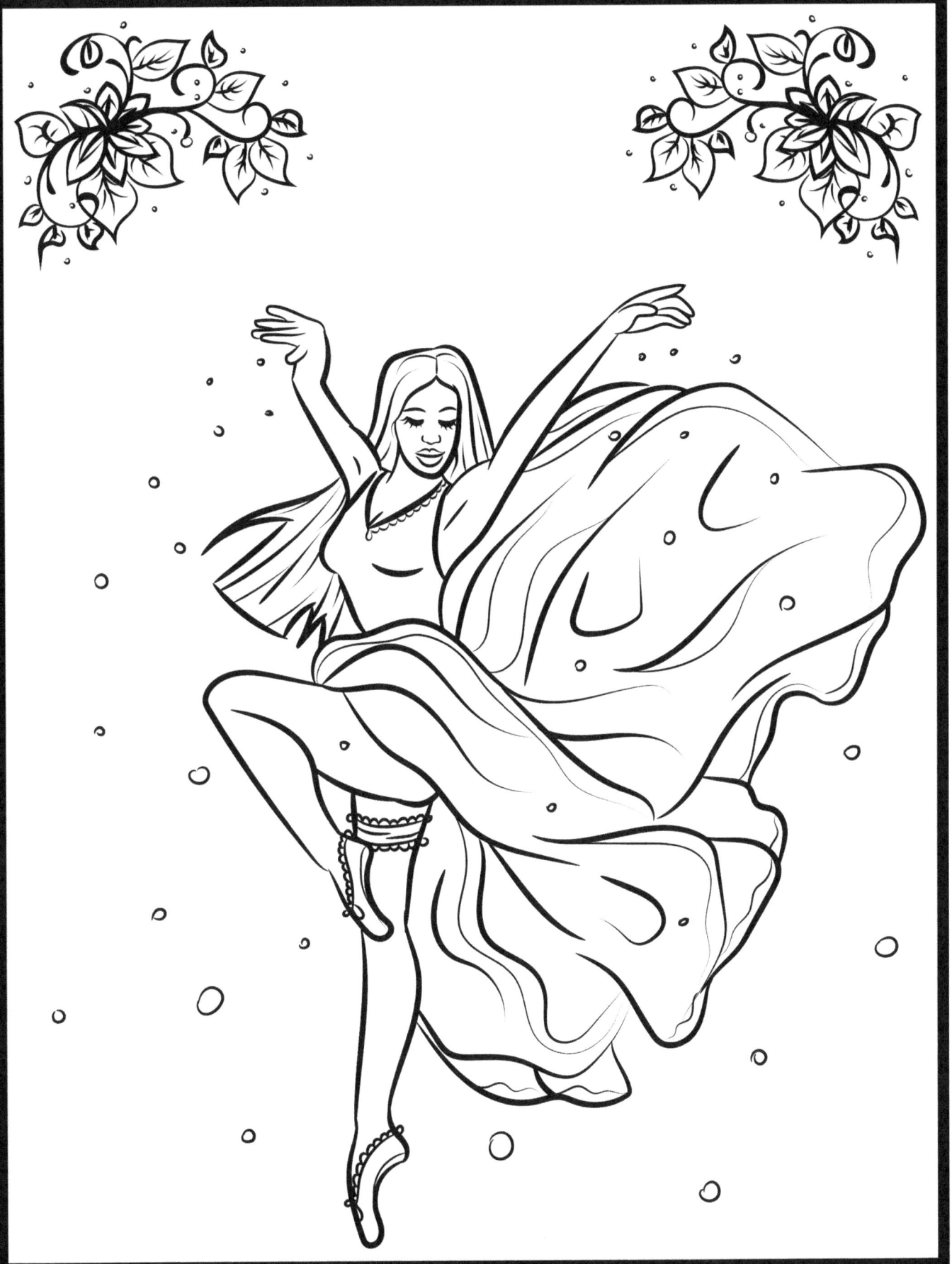

Icy steps

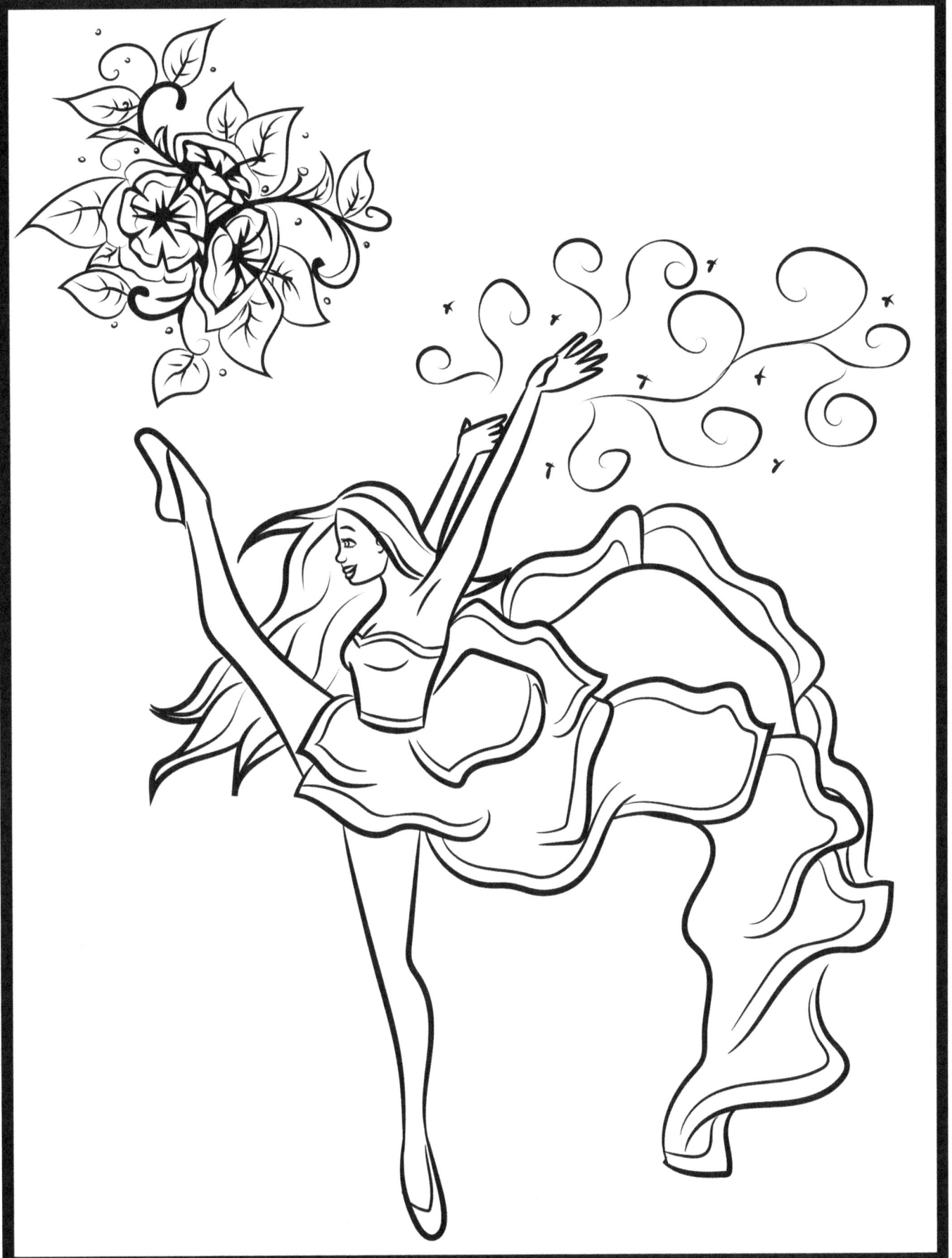

Happy Sparkle

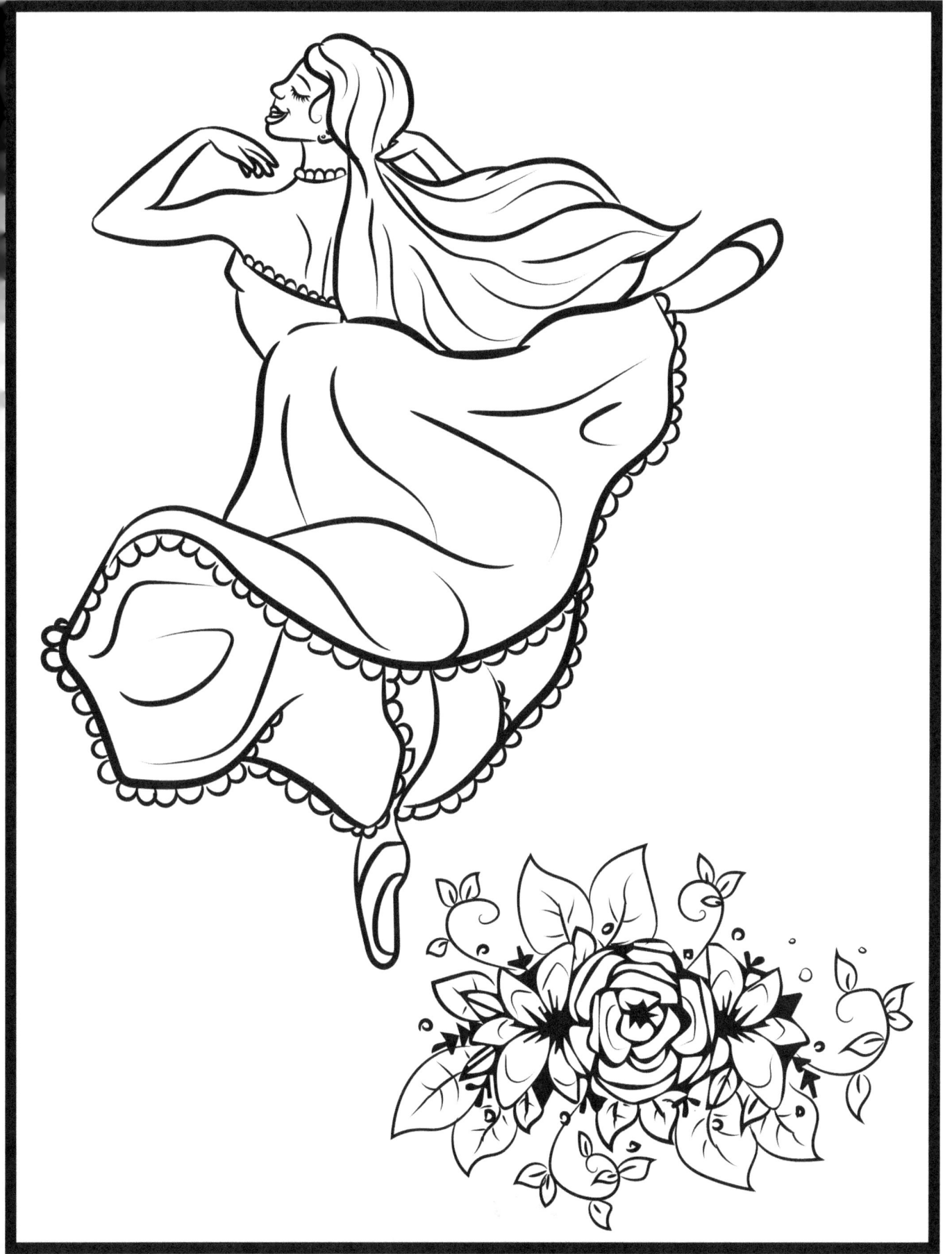

Elegant Waltz

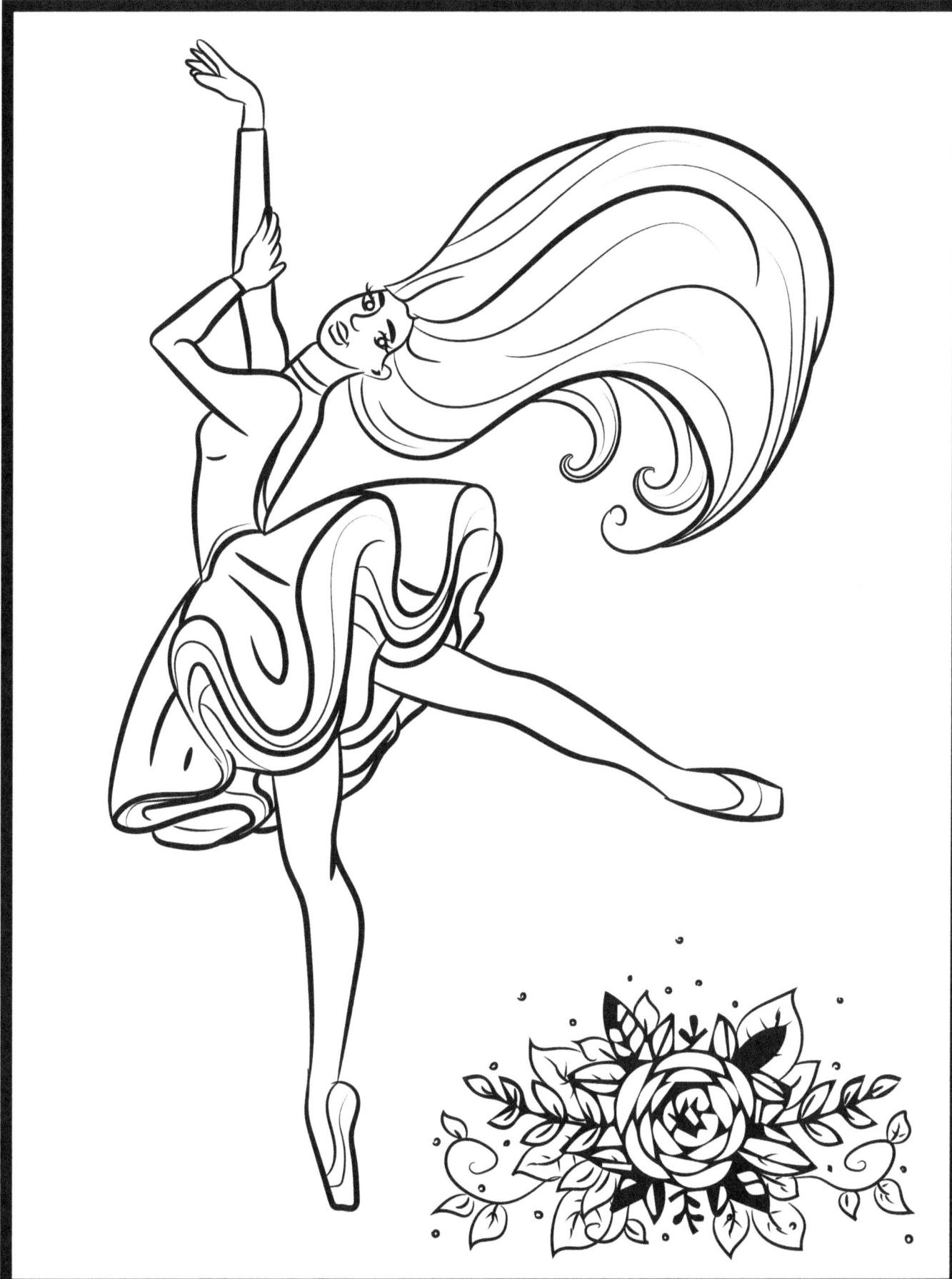

Summer's Pirouette

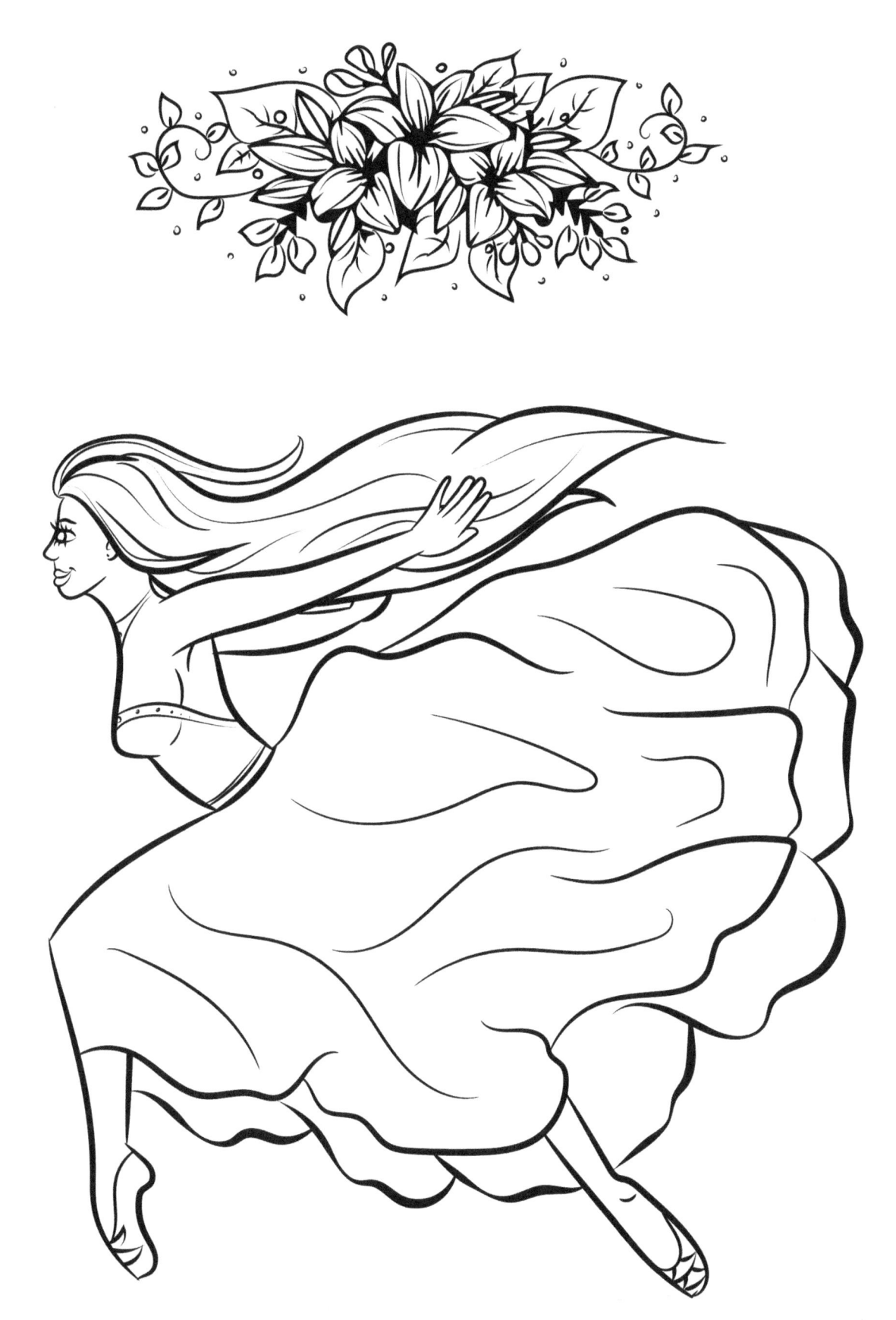

I Take the Lead

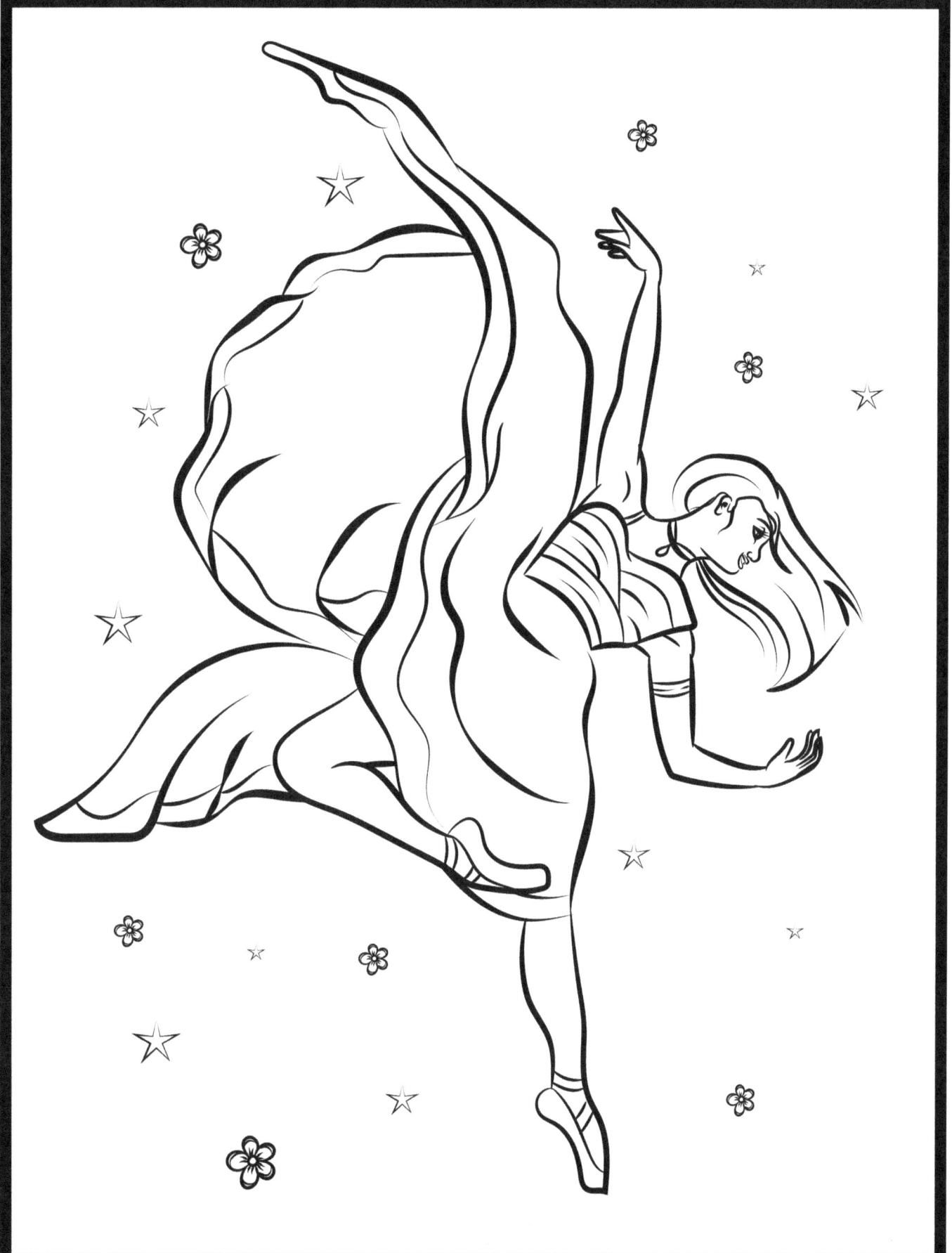

Floating Dream

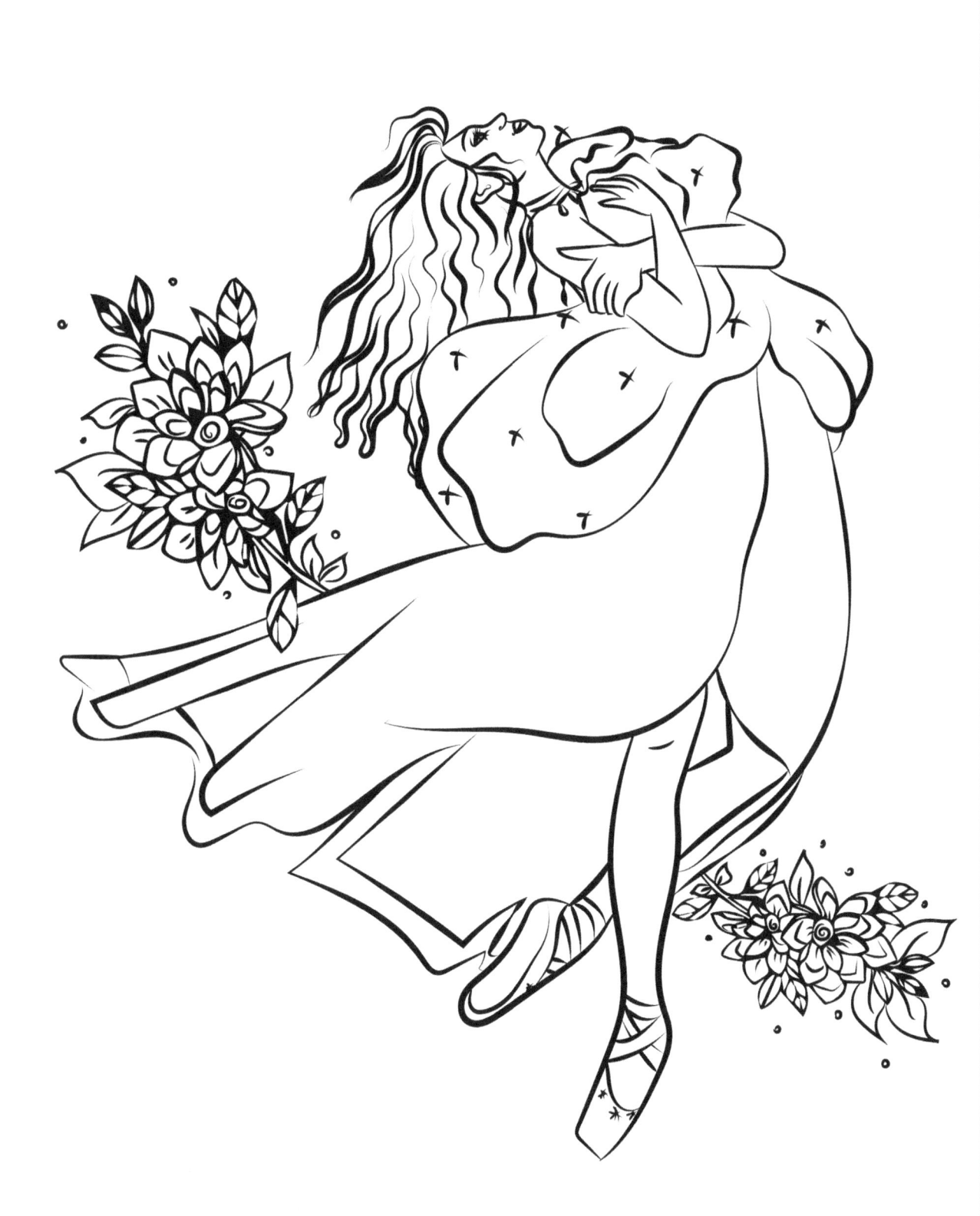

Divine Embracing

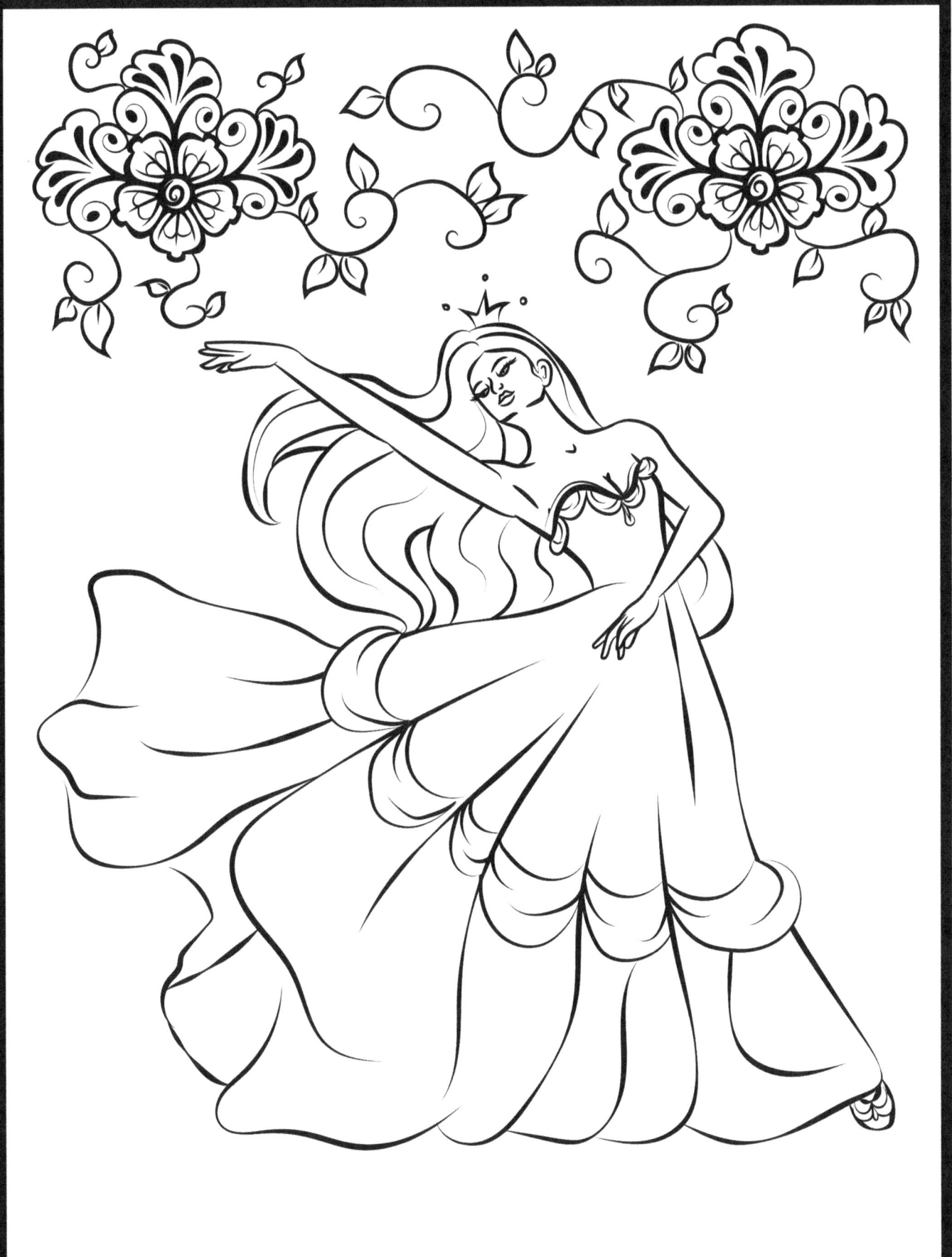

Flower Princess

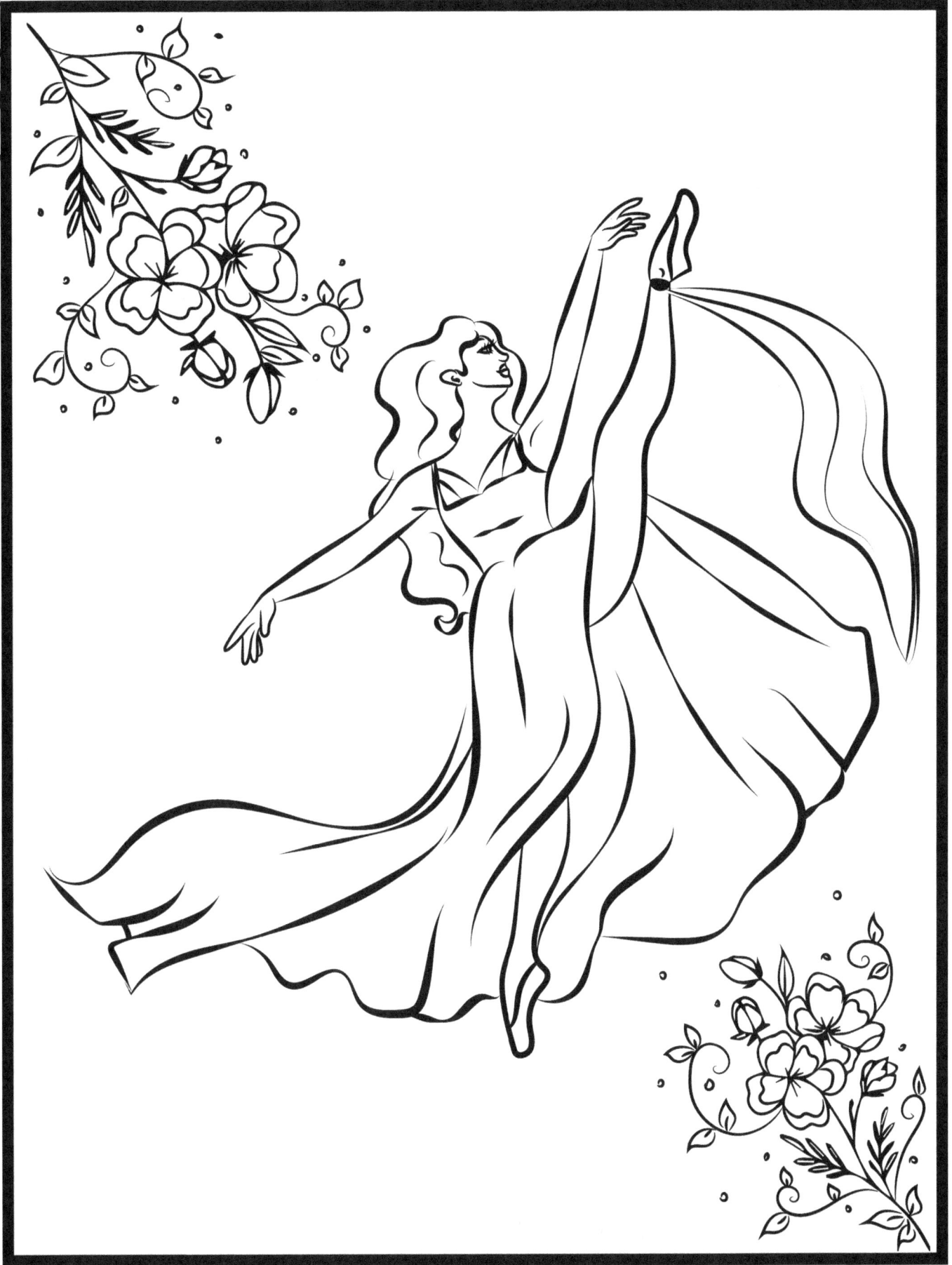

Dance of Freedom

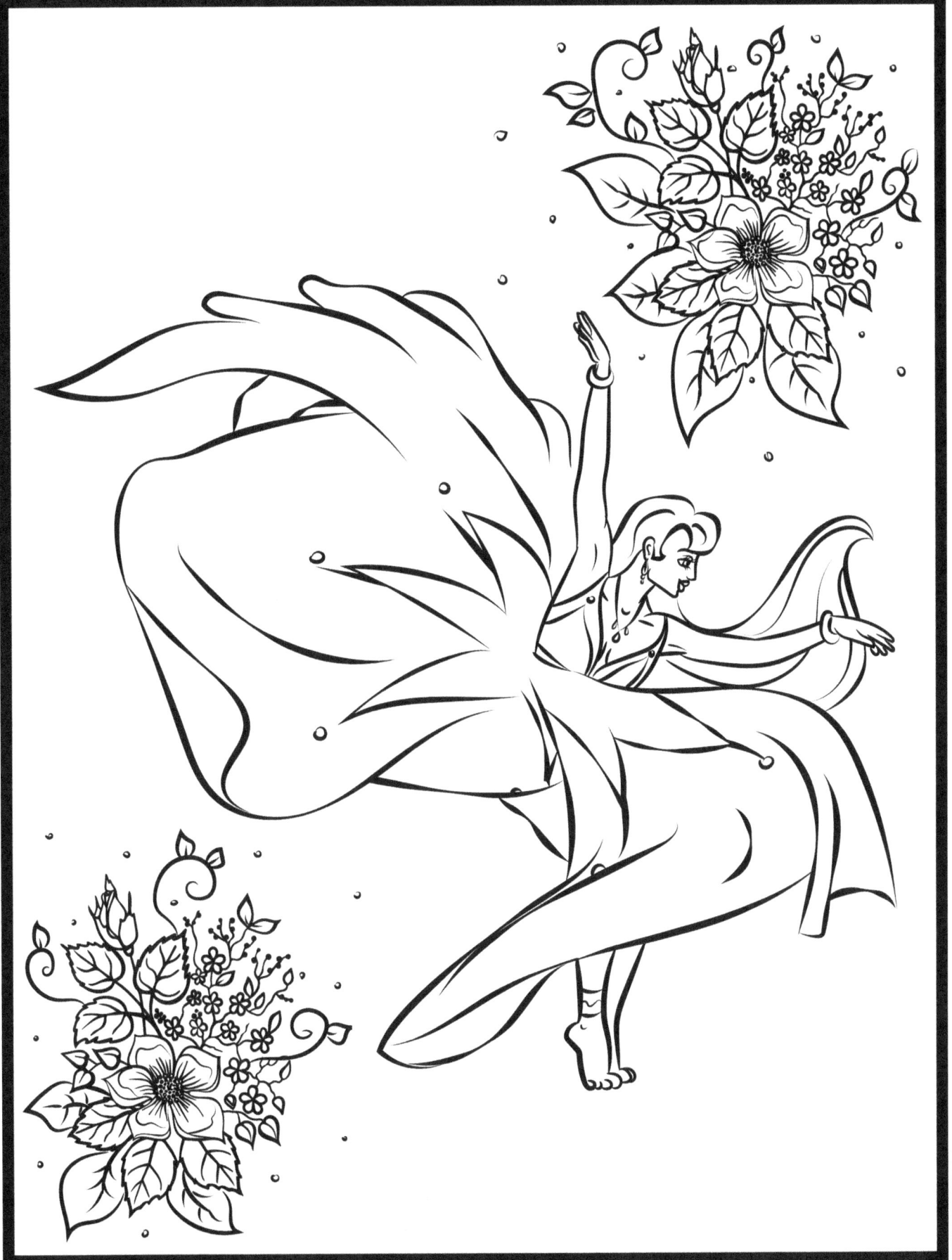

Dance with Me!

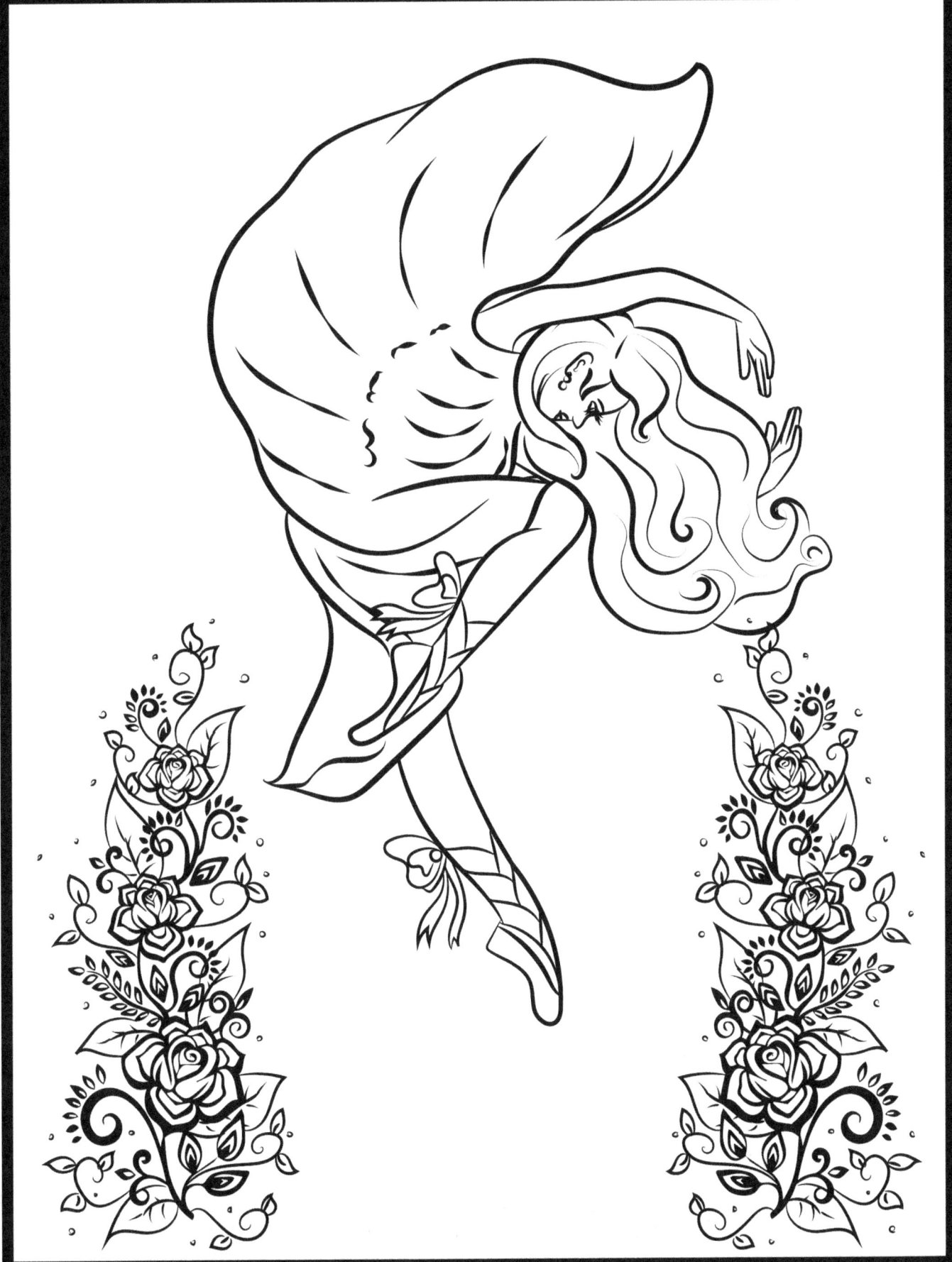

The Soul's Choreography

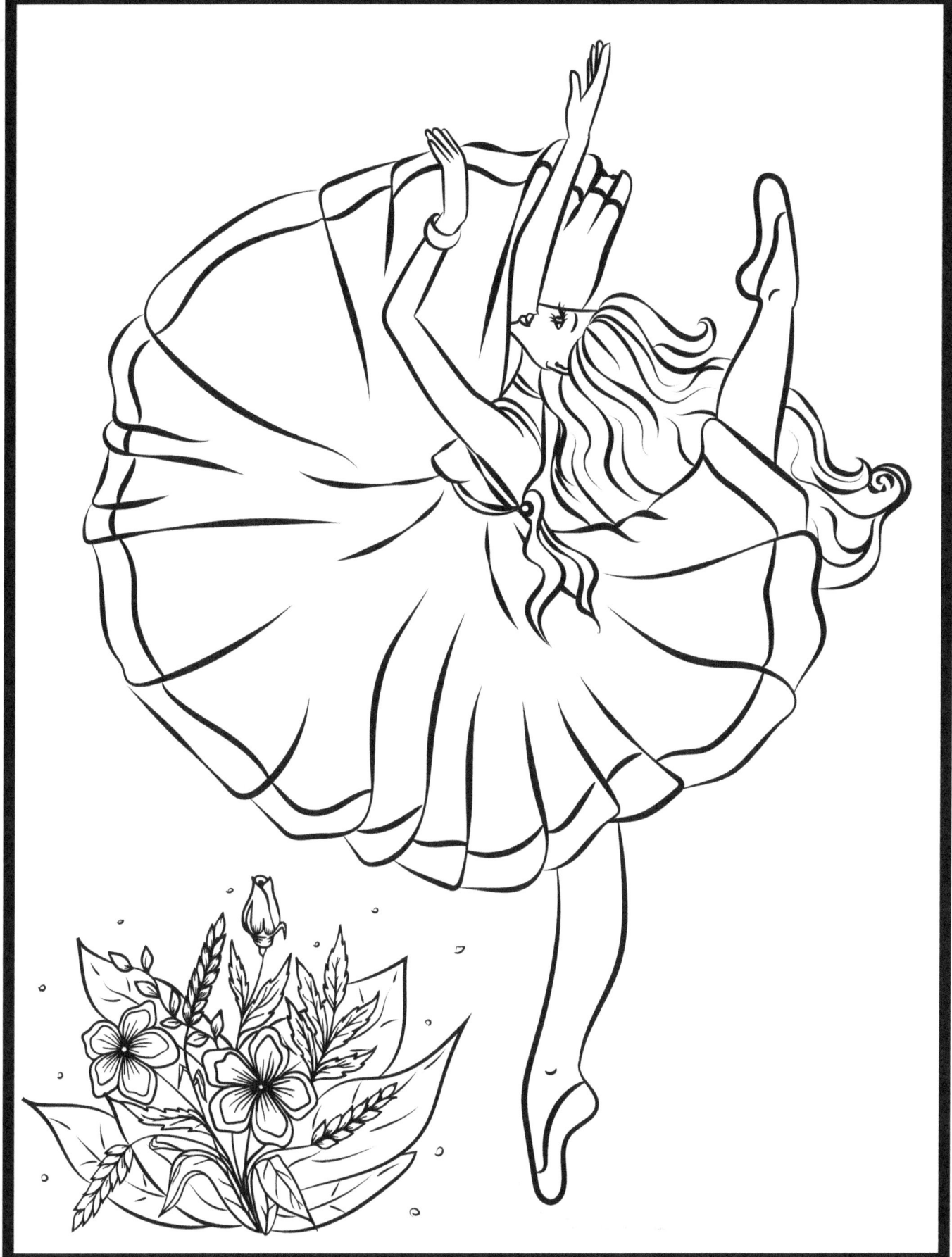

See Me Dancing

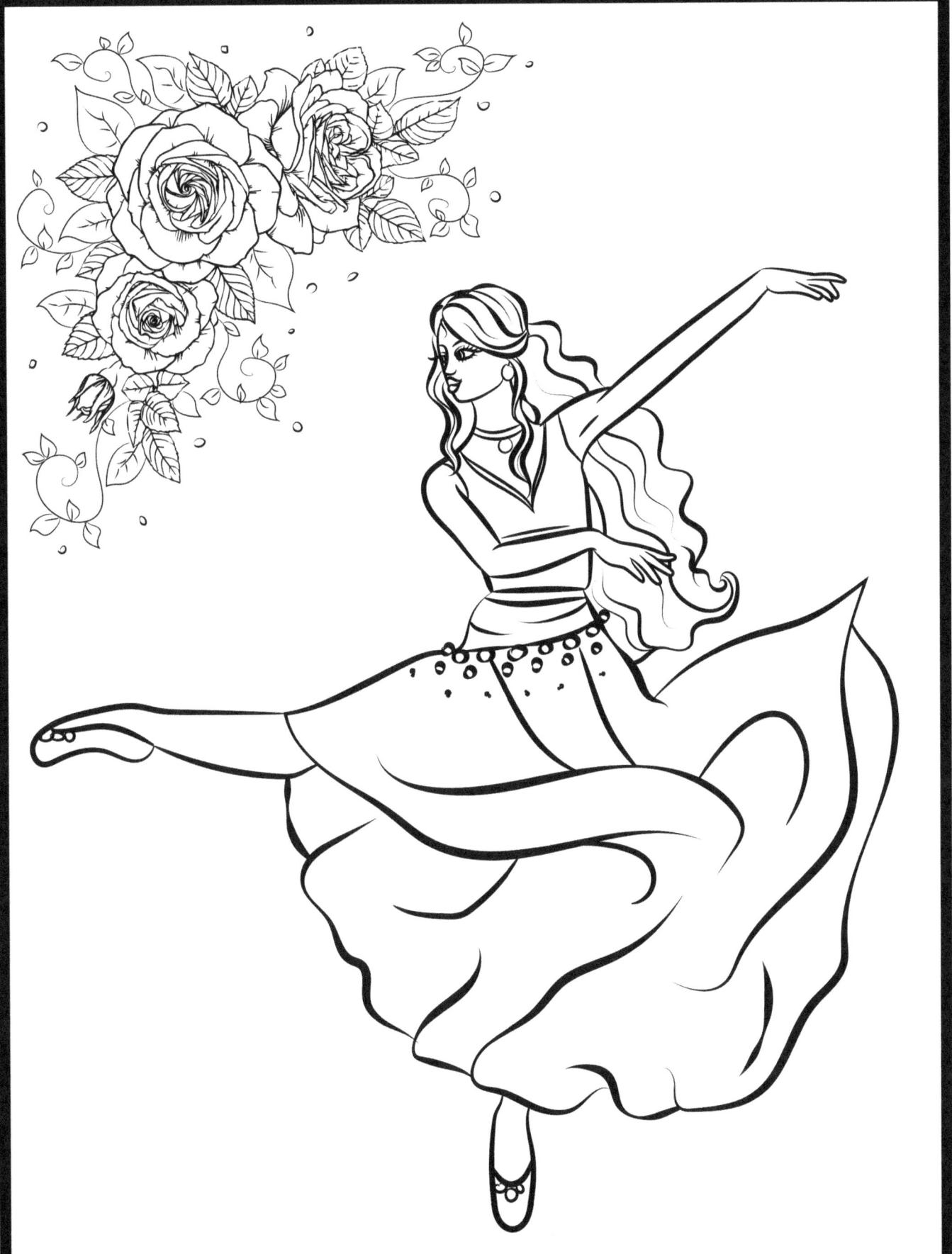

Perfect Pirouette

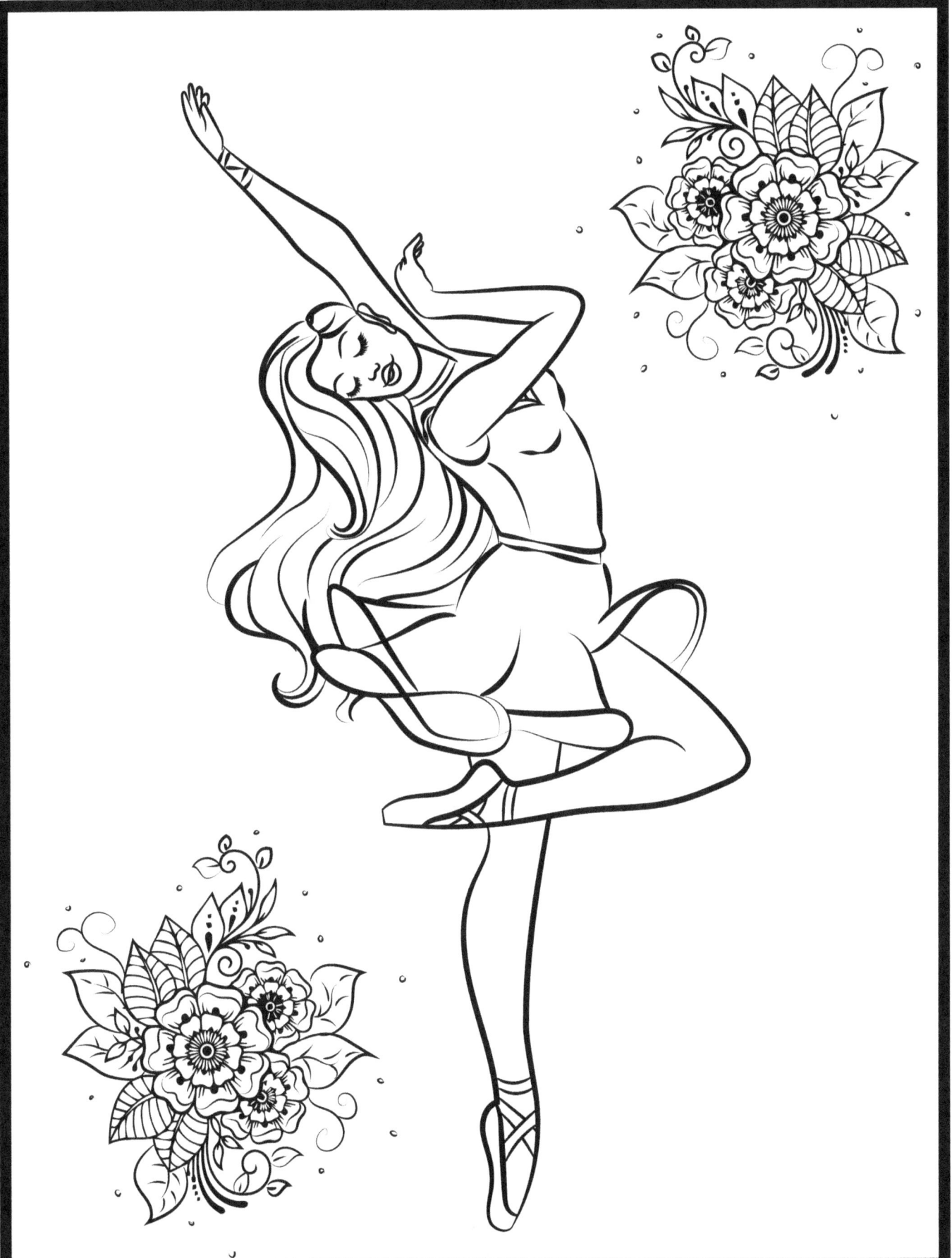

Tender Rhythm

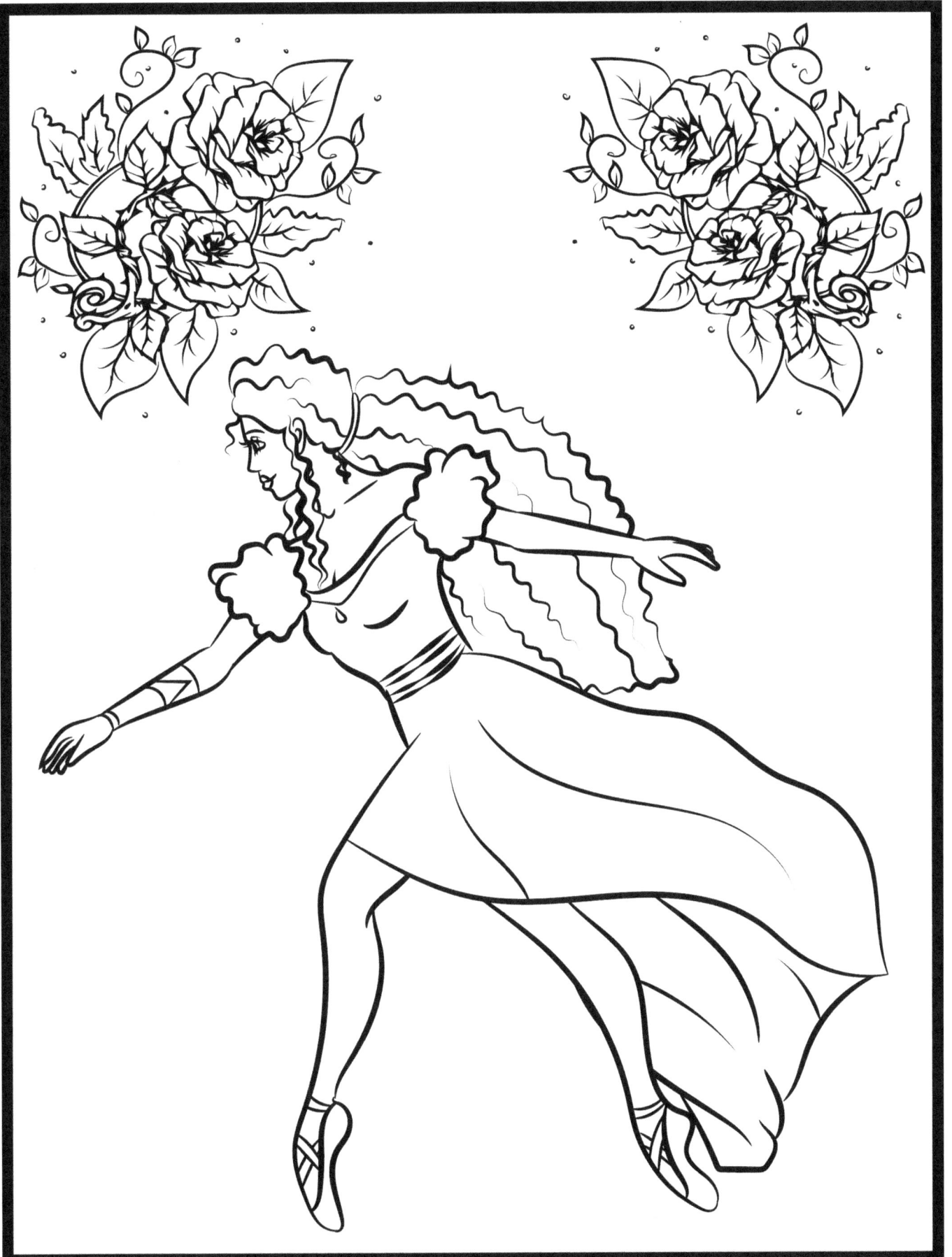

Confident Steps

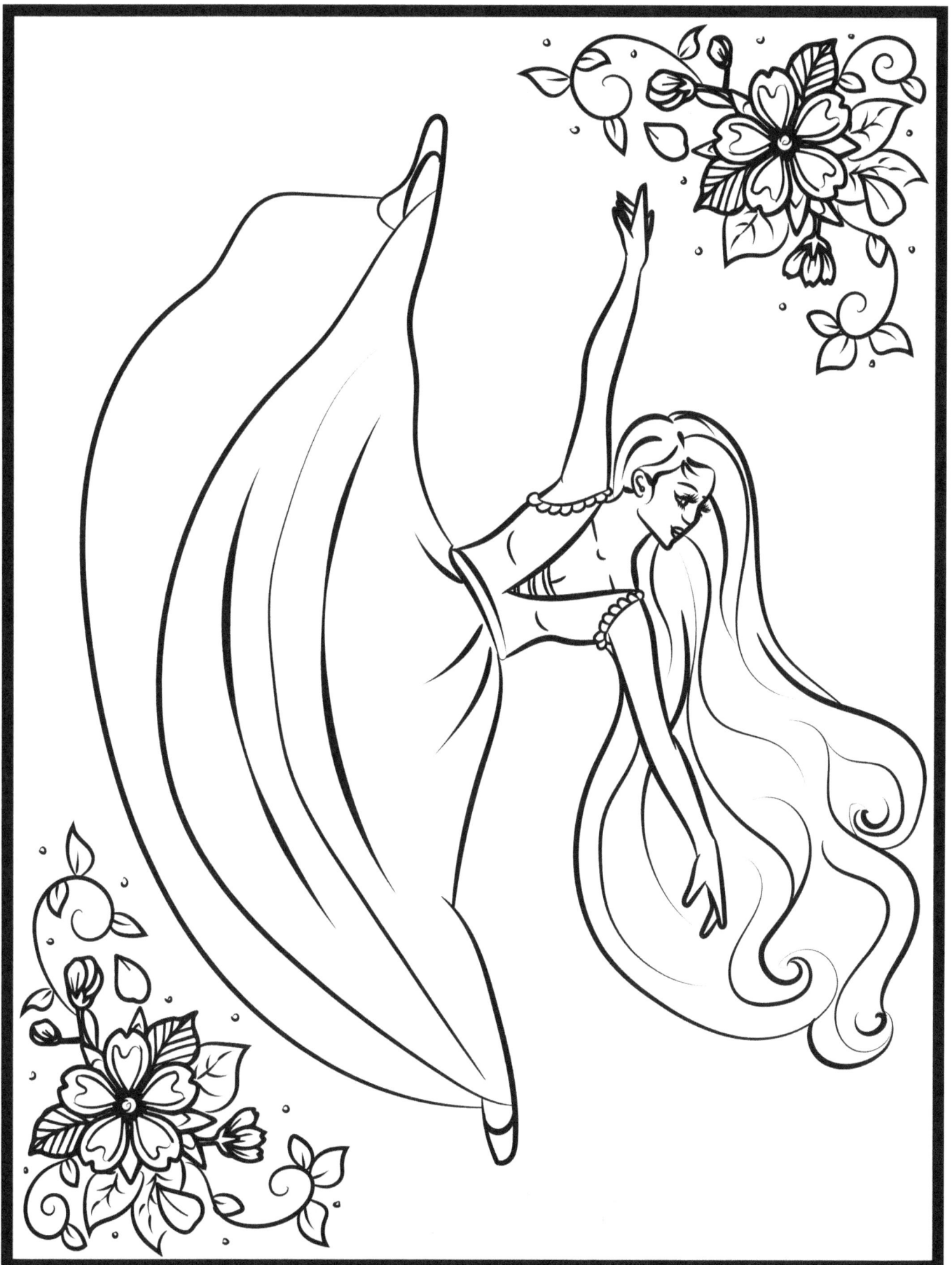

Flexible Beauty

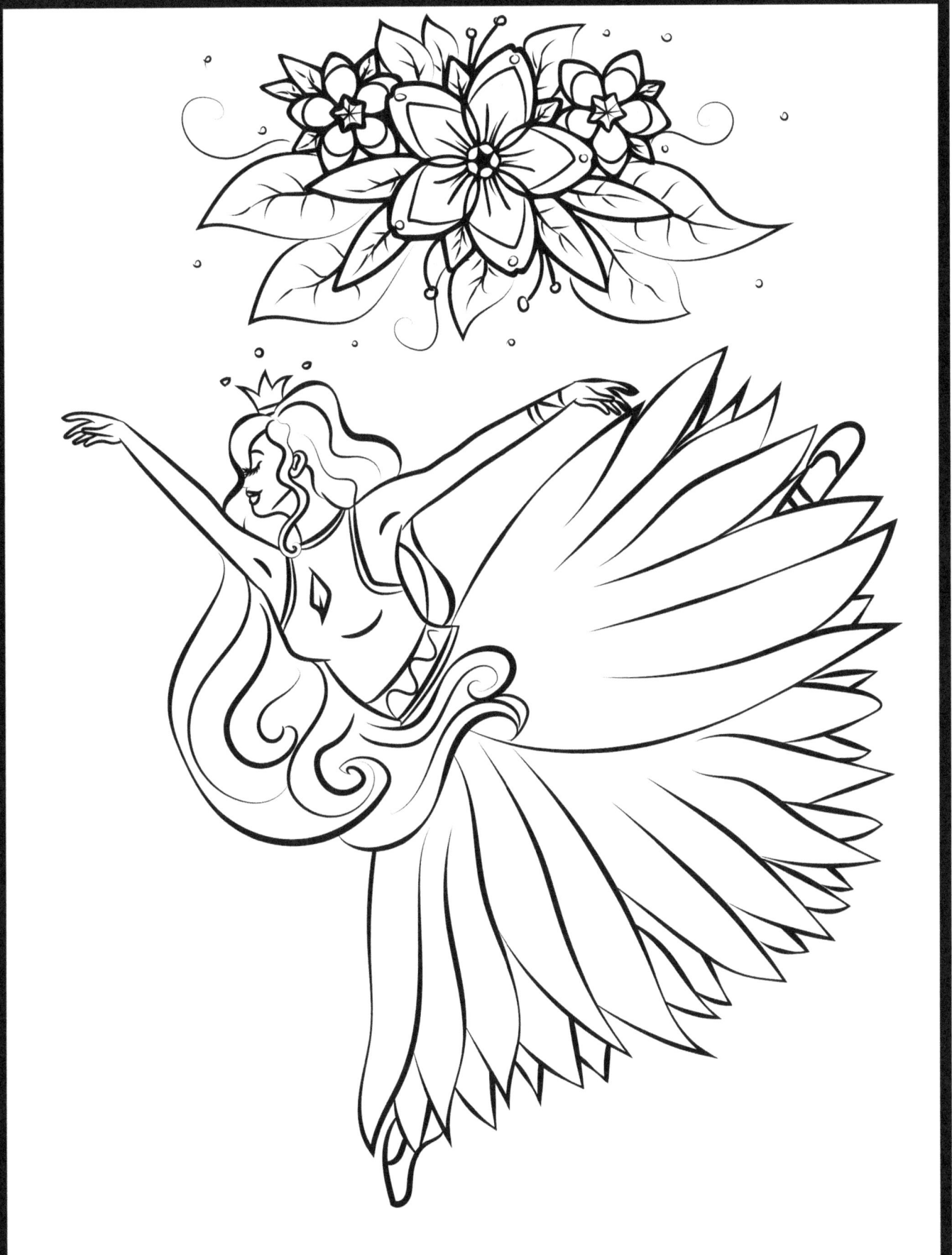

Flower Dress

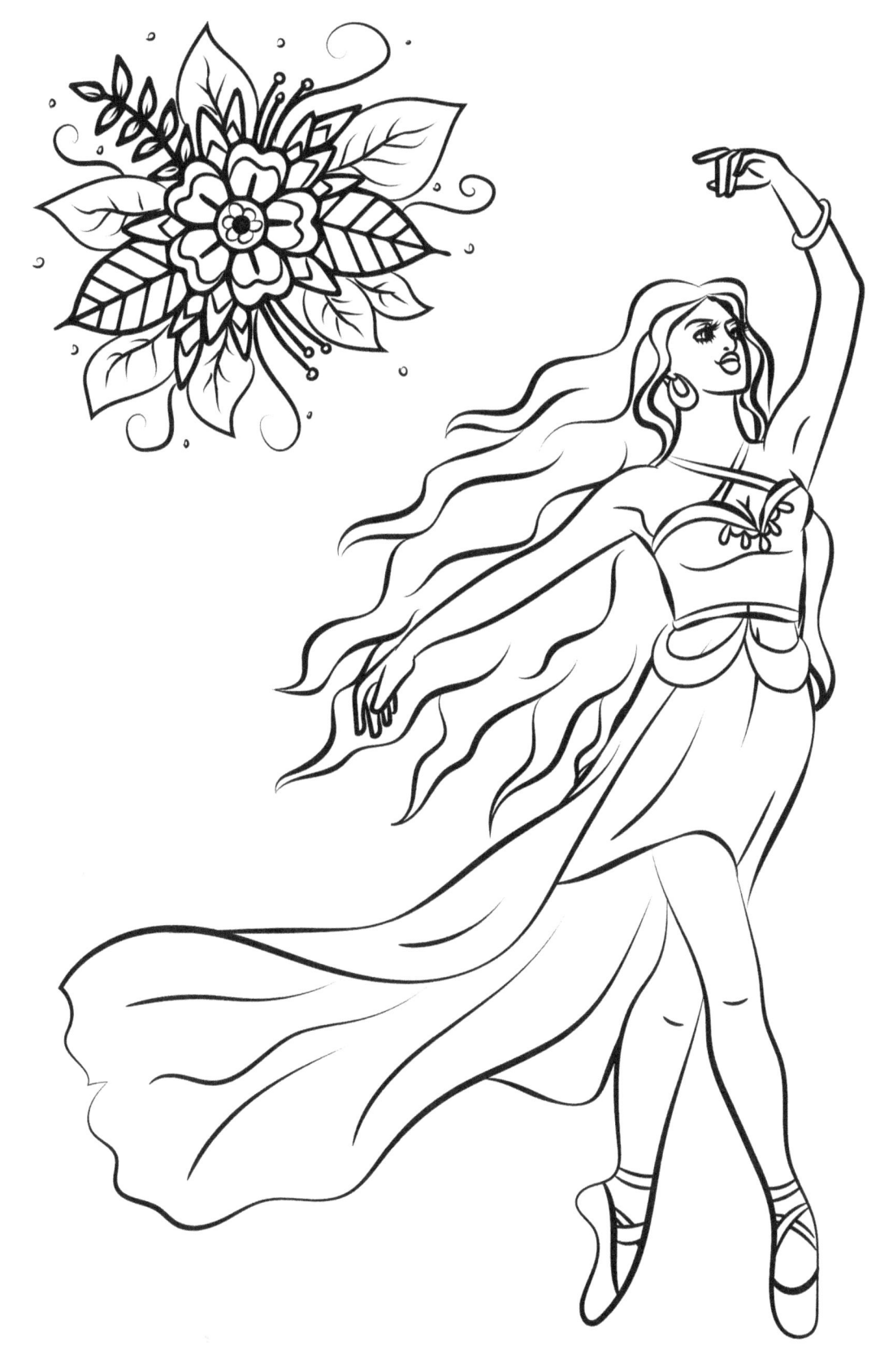

"Beauty of Liberty"

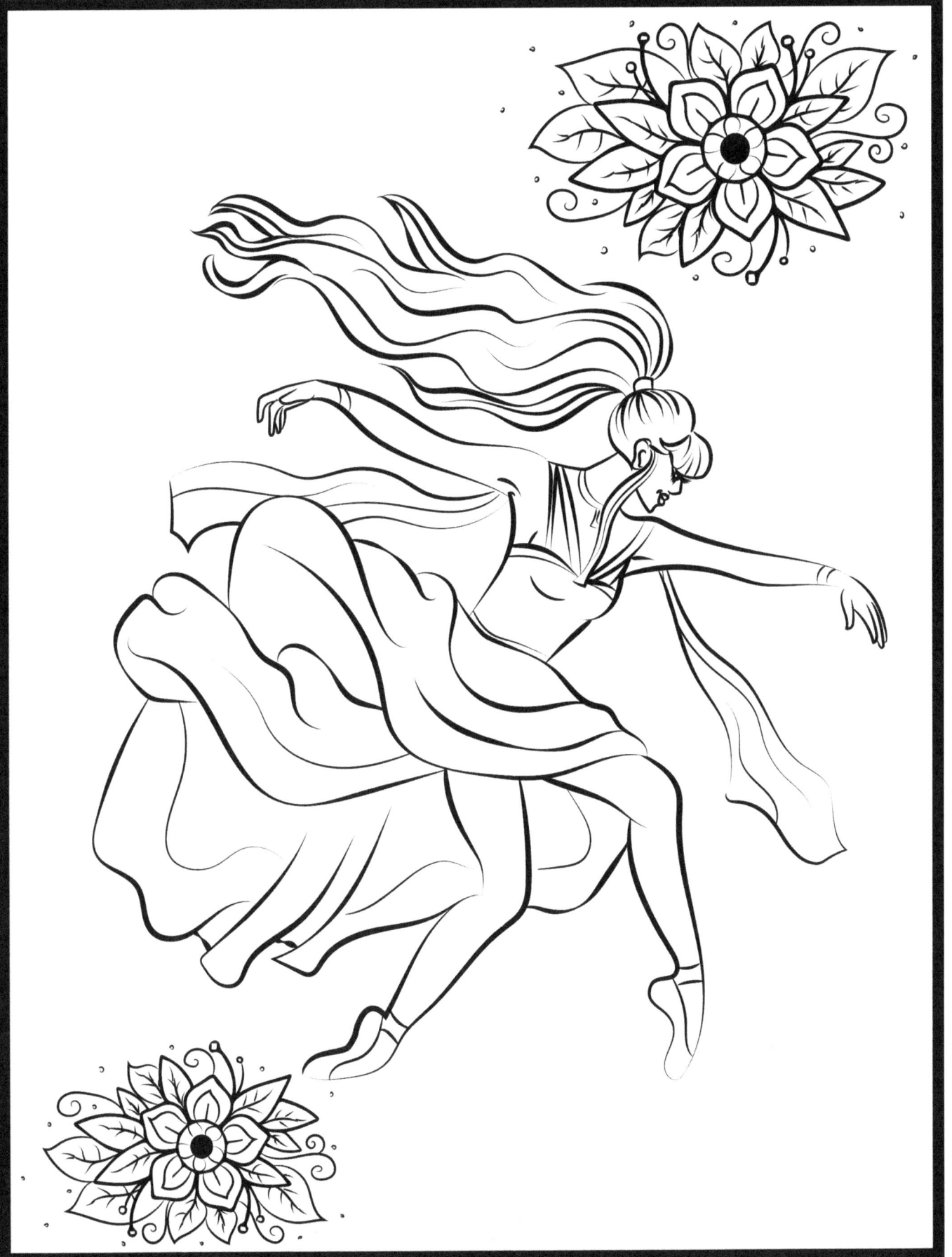

Ponytail Style

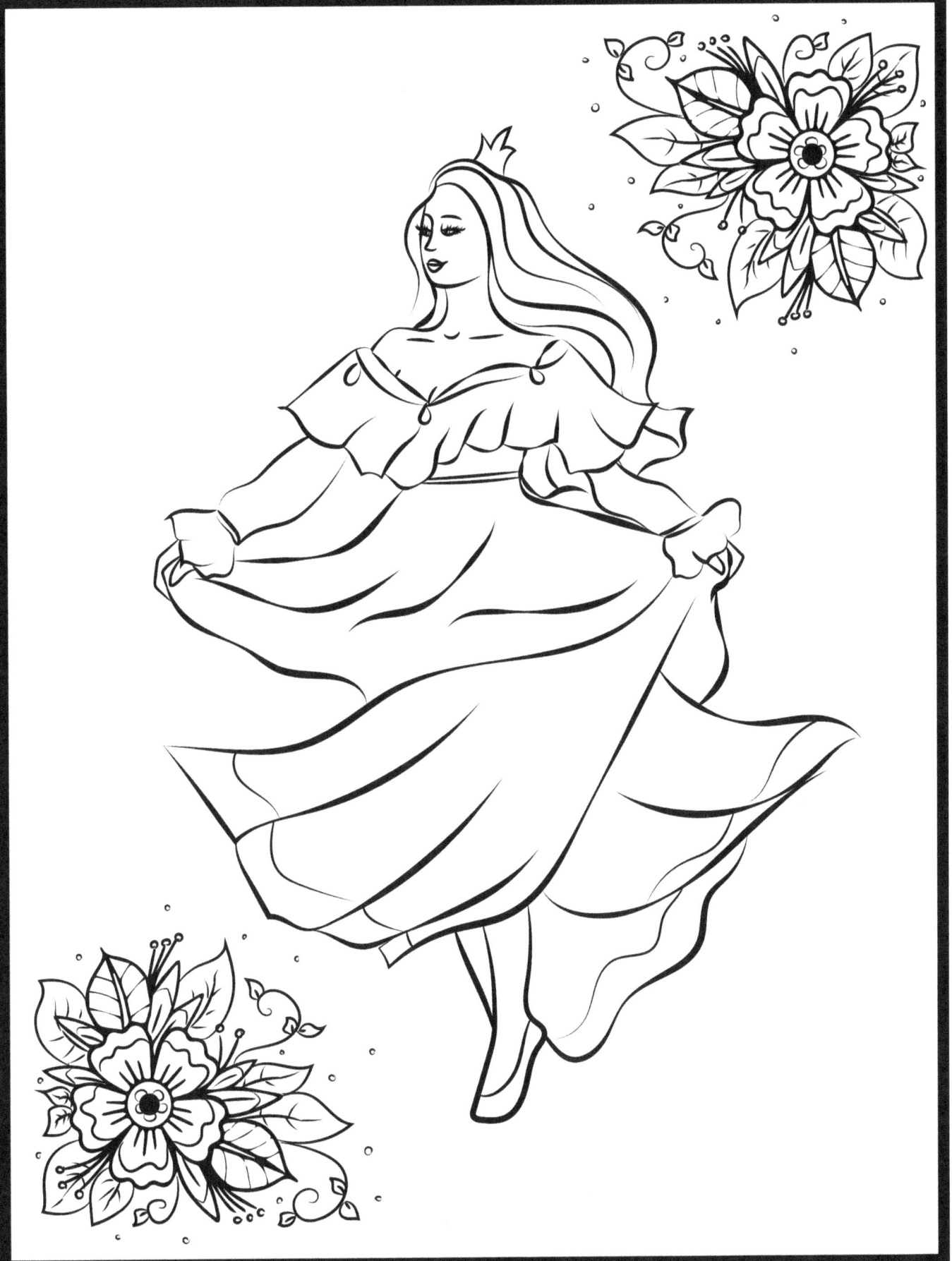

Noble Pulse

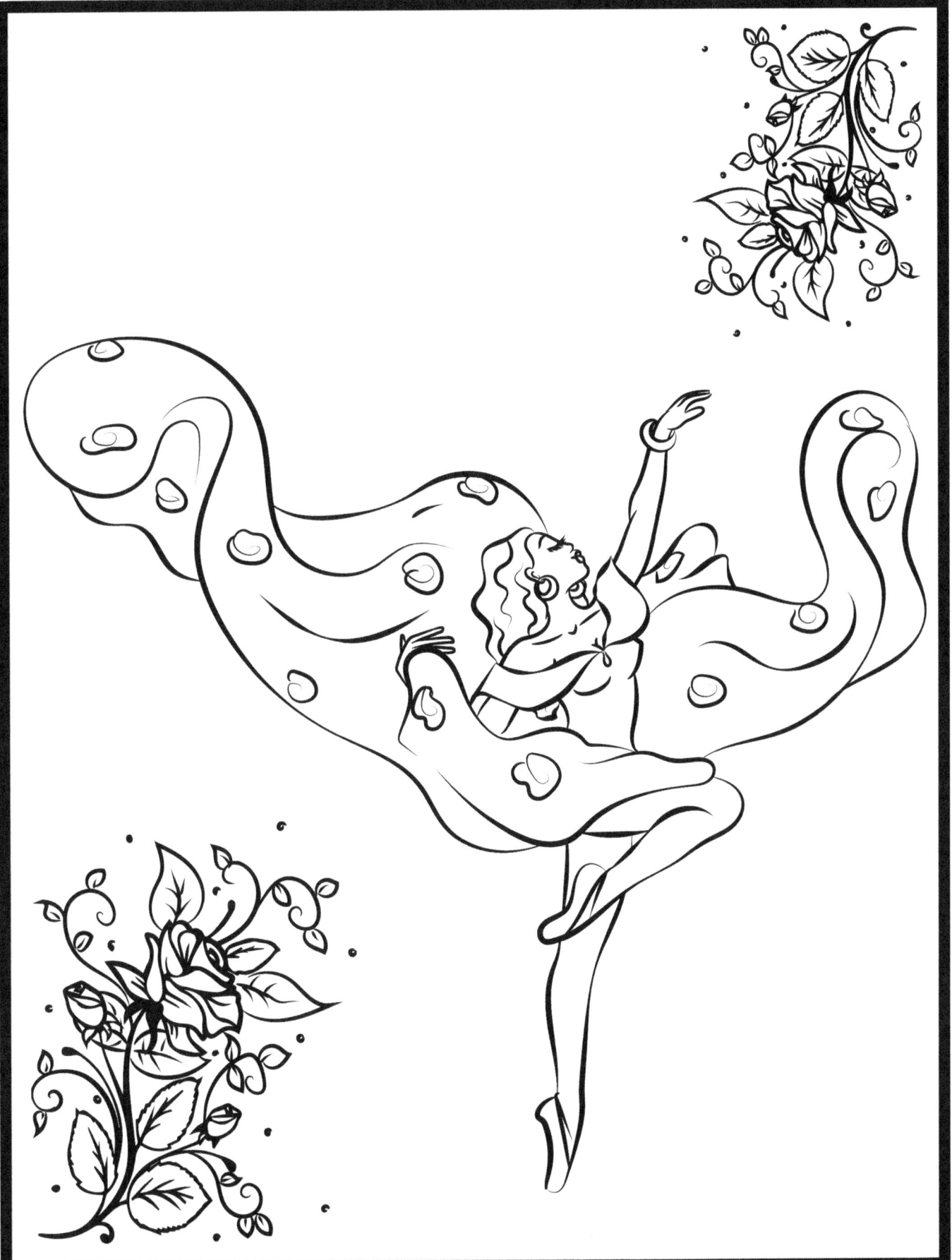

Rosie Pattern

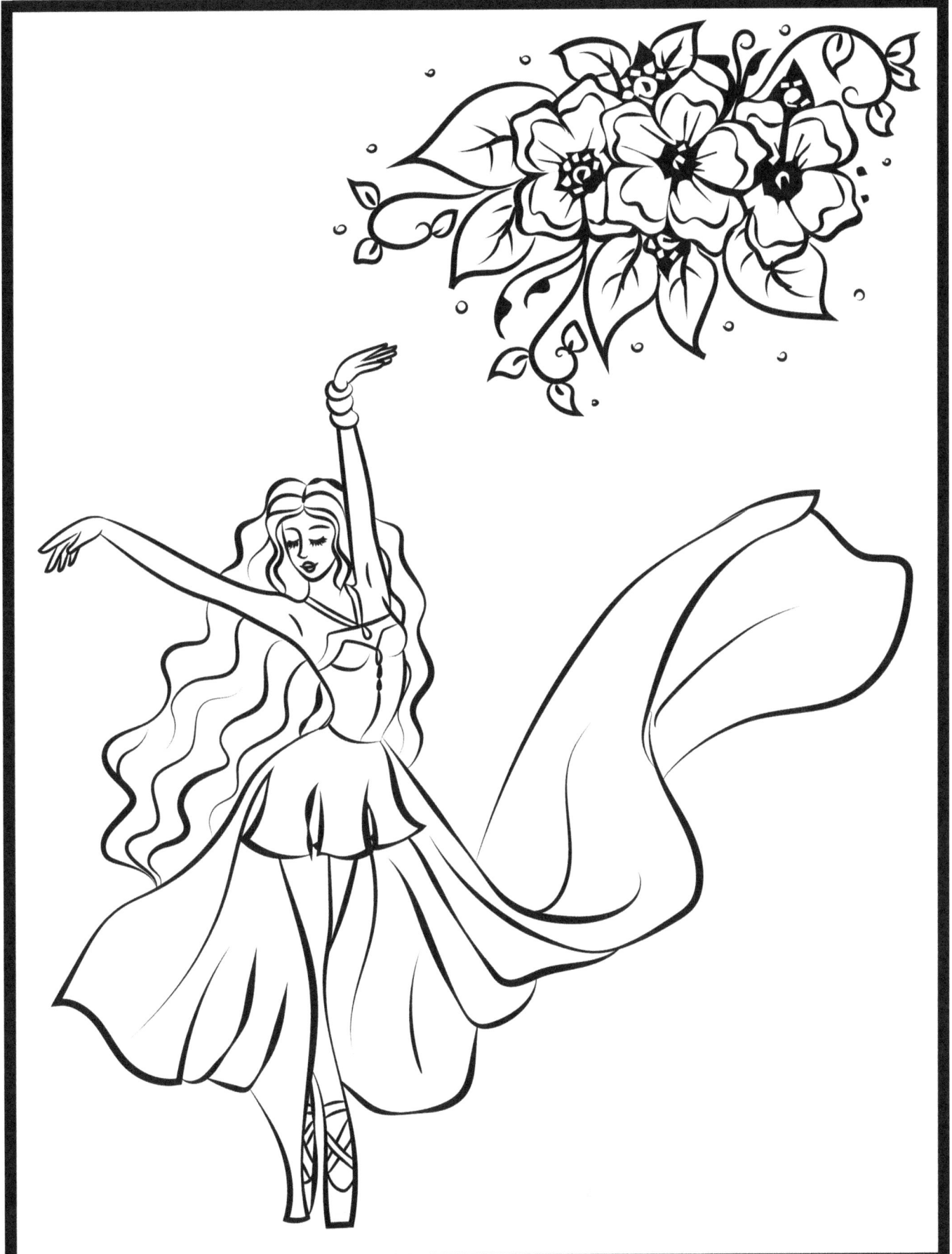

Tall Dancer

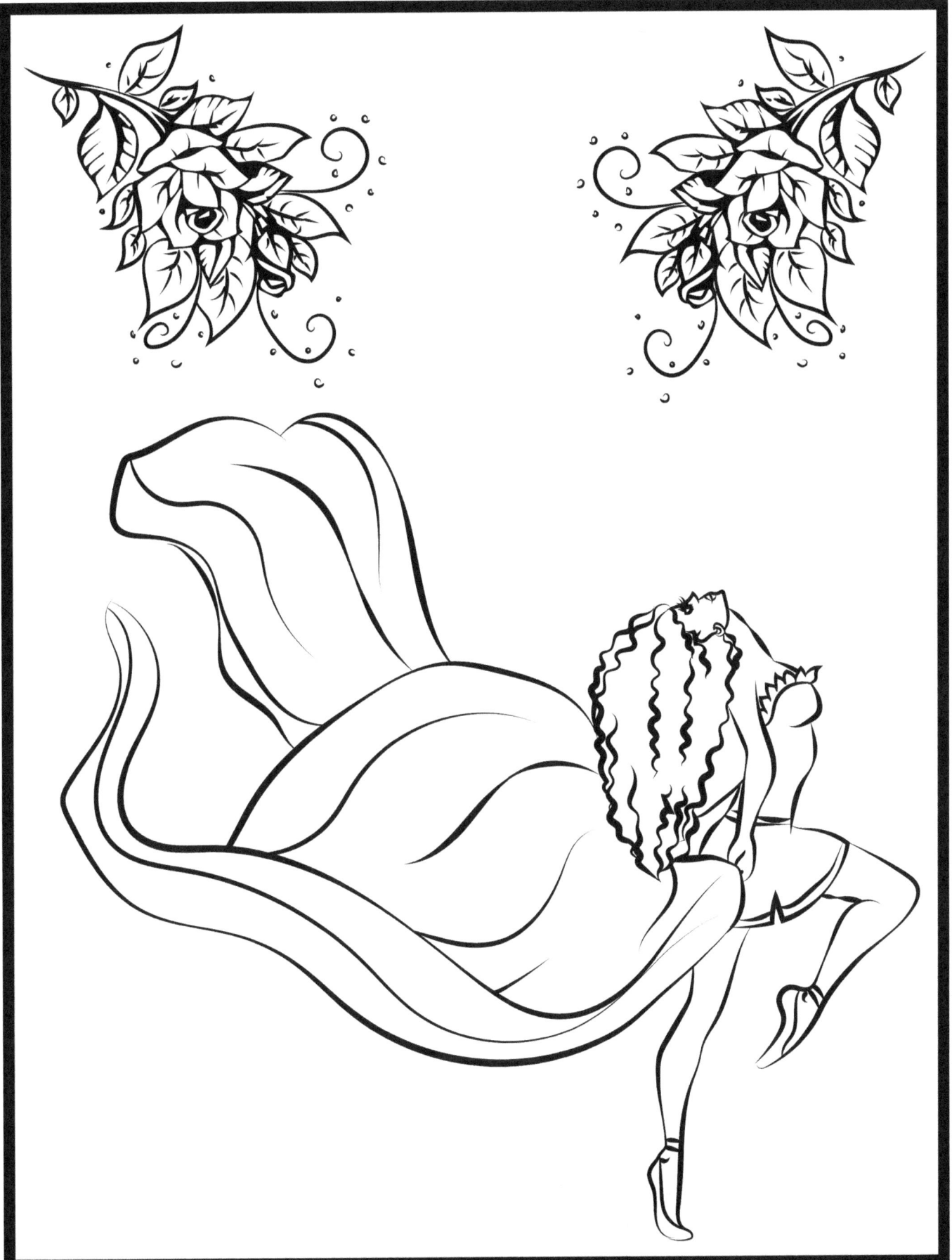

Sound of the Wind

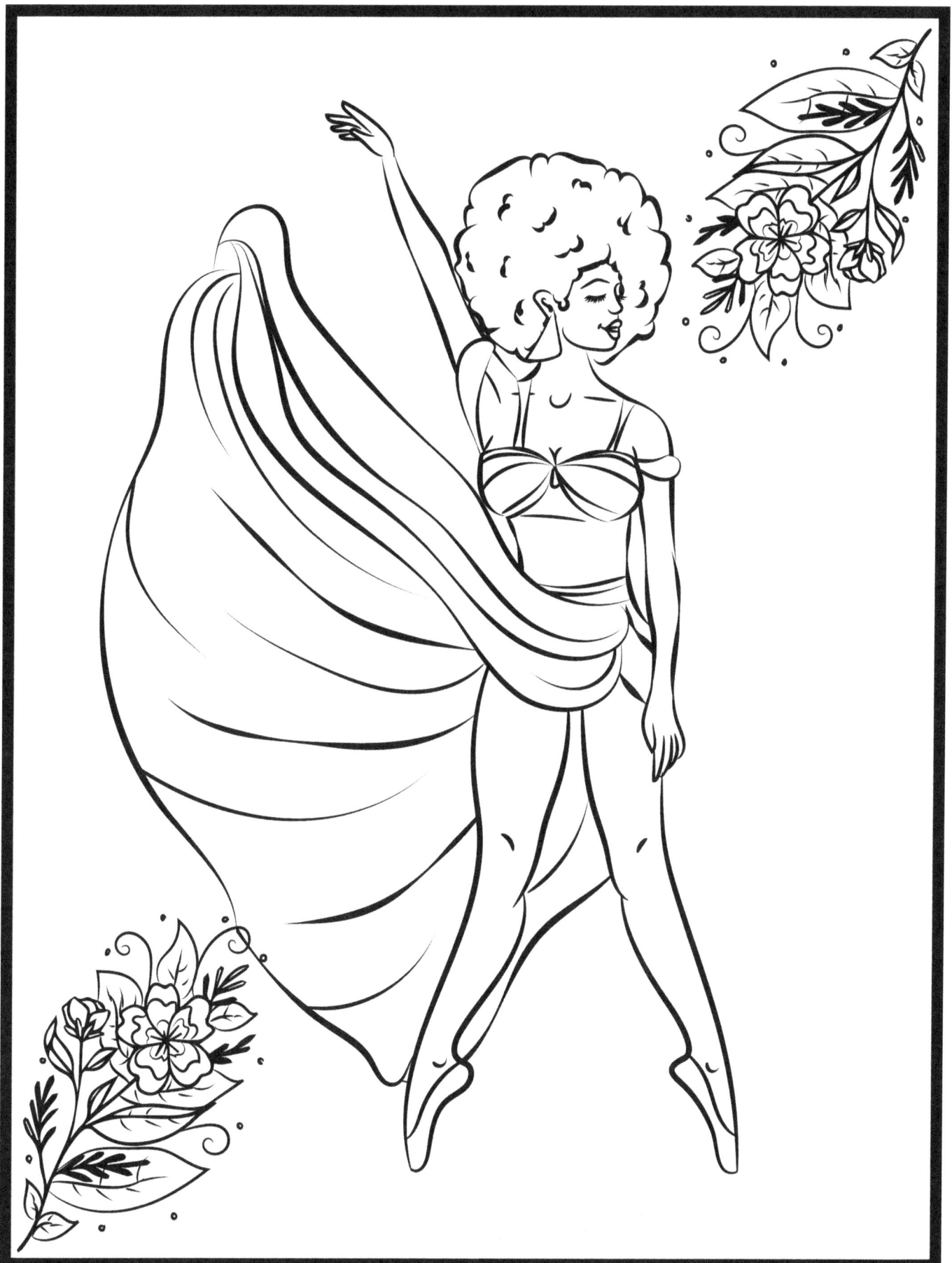

African-American Vibes

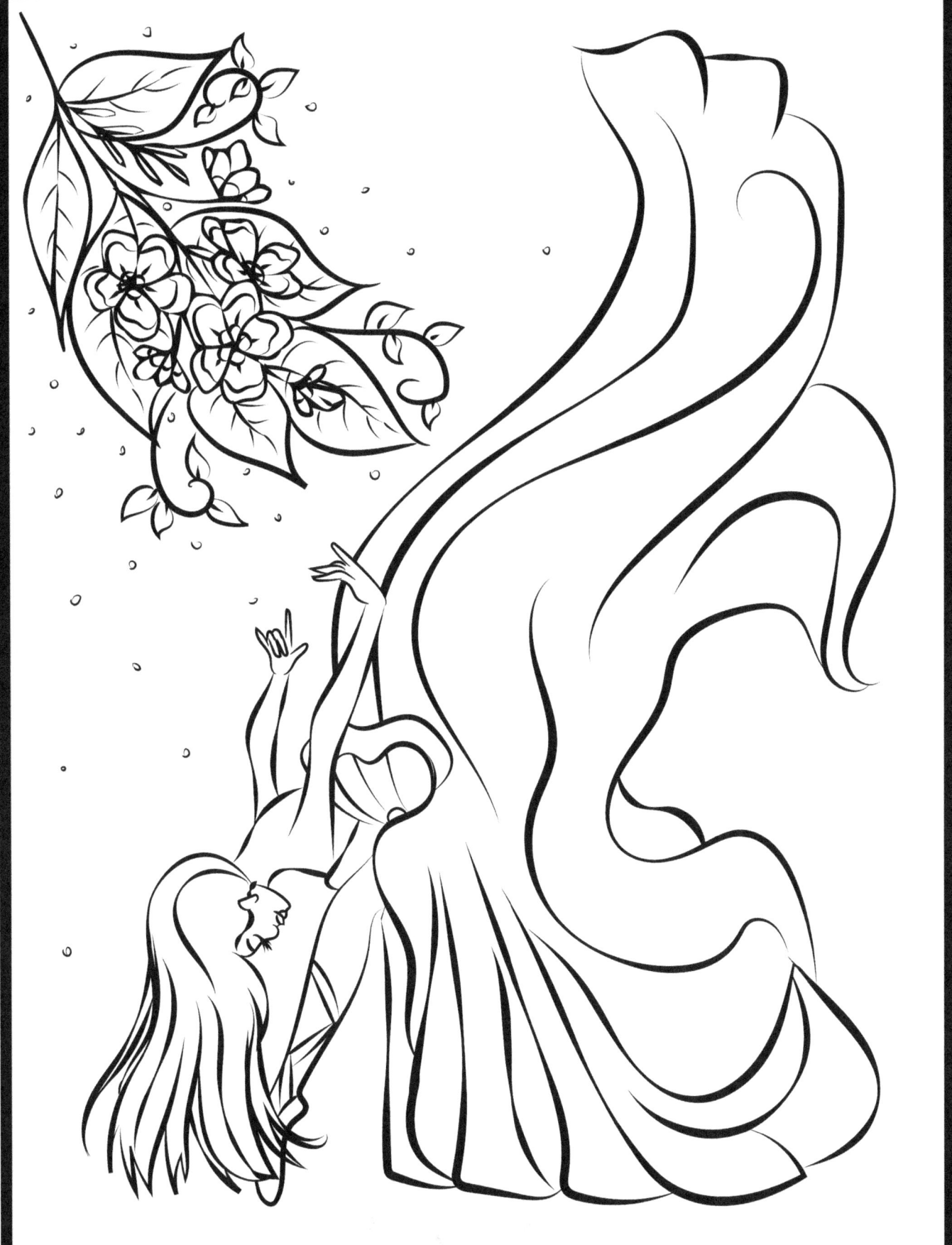

Thank you!

www.ingramcontent.com/pod-product-compliance
Lightning Source LLC
Chambersburg PA
CBHW081500220526
45466CB00008B/2732